The Leader's Supplement

The Leader's Supplement

A major platform for high performance leadership

Emmanuel Goshen

Published by Edson Consultancy

ISBN 978-0-993-06613-9

Printed and bound in the United Kingdom

Contents

About The Book

The leader's supplement is a professional guide which enables leaders and managers to equip themselves with the right and prefect knowledge of effective performance. The book simplifies the basic parameters required in making strategic planning and execution a reality, such as building, maintaining and encouraging a high performance leadership within an organisation. Readers would discover more on how best to utilize their strength for the benefit of their teams and organisations.

About The Author

Emmanuel Goshen is the founder of Edson Consultancy, a coaching and training company for managers and senior executives, based in London. Goshen specializes in coaching strategy and leadership courses at board level. He holds a Masters level qualification in strategic management and leadership and is also a chartered manager at the Chartered Management Institute UK. Over the past eight years, Goshen has coached executives, mostly within the third sector, on how to improve performance and strategy in attaining a better direction, mostly in a fast-changing business environment. He is also a motivational and inspirational speaker who believes in the principles of rising above limitations and displacing obstacles to achieve desired and excellent results.

Goshen is the bestselling author of THE LEADER'S DIET, an informative and inspiration read.

I would like to dedicate this page to Almighty God,
the foundation and pillar of wisdom.

I would like to dedicate this page to my family and friends all over the world, most especially my mother, whom made me understand that responsibility has no other meaning other than, "being up and equal to challenges in one's life.

PREFACE

Having been successful with my first book, THE LEADER'S DIET, which happens to be an informative and inspirational read according to some readers, I considered it a point of responsibility to expatiate the basic principles and attributes of leadership. I took insight from the definition of a supplement, which has been referred to as an extra element required for completing or enhancing a particular target. Solely being a leader or attaining a leadership position by merit or opportunity is not sufficient. Having the right characteristics, features, and attributes is what makes one an effective leader and sets him or her apart from the rest, which is the main focus of THE LEADER'S SUPPLEMENT.

In the medical world, the major function of a supplement represents its ability to serve as a remedy for the deficiencies in a person's diet. However, LEADERSHIP WITHOUT PERFORMANCE IS INCOMPLETE; in other words, any leader who lacks the ability to deliver an expected result for organisational stakeholders within a specified time frame, would only be seen as an *icicle,* which pretends to be real during winter but finds it difficult to retain its position during summertime. As essential nutrients and vitamins play a huge role in redeeming poor digestion, hormone imbalances, weight loss programs, stress, and obesity for the purpose of a good quality of life, so does performance in leadership, because it reflects what a leader can do.

In a nutshell, performance leadership is the main platform for leading and managing an organisation towards success. It's about focusing on every valuable component to create value for all stakeholders. It aims at getting things done easier, better, faster, and more cost-effectively.

Performance leadership can be achieved by clarifying strategic priorities, building a shared sense of vision and purpose throughout an organisation, developing commitment, motivation, and establishing effective collaboration.

Ensuring the translation of strategic priorities into operations, building operational programmes, and capabilities for driving effective management, is another outcome of performance leadership, which enables leaders to remain highly effective. The use of a comprehensive approach to business intelligence to support decision-making, innovation, and continuous learning are major platforms in making leaders highly effective as well.

Performance leadership is a systematic, results-oriented approach to management and leadership for high-performing organisations, teams, and individuals. The approach consolidates the fundamentals of management and leadership within an organisation, and then builds on clients' existing abilities by increasing the rigour, range, and effectiveness of their capabilities.

High-performance leadership can be achieved through the introduction of best-practice processes, tools and techniques, together with the development of skills and competencies, brought together within an integrated system. However, the system needs to focus on three parameters, or major capabilities:

Organisational Development, which focuses on the development of core processes and associated tools and techniques that are fundamental to a performance-leading organisation. This is also known as organisational capability.

People Development, which focuses on the development of core competencies, attitudes and behaviours that are fundamental to leading, managing and performing in a performance-leading organisation.

Knowledge Development, which focuses on the development of core business intelligence to underpin the quality of all decision-making in a performance-leading organisation. It also deals with how improvements are sustained in terms of knowledge sharing, innovation, and continuous learning within an organisation.

PREFACE

However, building and sustaining a high-performance leadership culture requires a well-coordinated and timely execution of strategy from others, which reflects a leader as being effective. It also requires time, patience, and a clear focus on what needs to be achieved within a time frame. Listening to what people expect from you as a leader, and then responding empathically, would improve your skills and knowledge dramatically towards being highly effective.

CHAPTER 1

INTRODUCTION TO HIGH-PERFORMANCE LEADERSHIP

A man's strength is not in the achievement of his wealth, influence, and power, but rather in the ability to sustain them on a long-term basis. However, success is often measured on long-term achievements, with the ability to maintain outstanding performance. The ability to plan ahead to achieve success, and to maintain it with the right principles and approaches, reflects the strength of a leader in both the short and the long run.

I remember an African tale of two friends who were contracted by a wealthy man to remove the strong grasses and weeds from his farmland, for which they both requested a cutlass each. The two conditions for payment were the distance covered, and how clear the ground was. Having received a cutlass each, one of the men was able to discern that his cutlass wasn't very sharp, and would not help him clear much ground in a short amount of time. He wisely went to sharpen it at the local blacksmith shop, but the other man never bothered to check his cutlass. When they both set out for the task, the wise one was able to clear a large amount of ground, while the other man struggled with the blunt cutlass, and as time progressed, he became increasingly frustrated. He decided to ask the wise man about the magic behind his cutlass. The moment he learned about the blacksmith, he immediately went there, only to find out that the blacksmith was out. He began to search for another blacksmith to sharpen his cutlass, which took a lot of time. Once the job was finished, he discovered that he didn't have enough money to pay for the work. He went back home to get money, and by the time he got back to the farmland, it was getting dark. He rushed to catch up, but only accomplished little work.

The wealthy man later returned to measure the distance cleared by each of the workers. He was happy with the wise man's work, and paid him a good amount of money; he also hired him to clear the rest of the farmland. Further, he employed him as the manager of the farm, which included livestock, crops, and other holdings. I am sure the wealthy man's decision was based on the wise man's keen observations and realism in knowing what to do at the right time. In truth, the wealthy man knew the cutlasses were blunt and needed to be sharpened, but he deliberately didn't tell the men ahead of time. The act of being consistent, observant, and realistic reflects the strength and other strong qualities of the wise one, which were the major components the rich man was seeking.

A well-known adage says that morning shows the day, but judgment comes by night. This was a popular saying of my secondary school principal, who happened to be a retired colonel in the army. After some years of hearing this saying, I asked my teacher to explain the saying's meaning in serious terms. I remember vividly how he looked me in the eye and replied that the achievement of every man is seen, assessed and judged at a later stage in his life, when making corrections and adjustments is a dead option. After every game, accountability follows. Decisions made at the early stage of one's life go a long way in determining one's position in his later years, because one either takes the praise or the blame. Nothing shows the real value of a man more than his previous achievements, because it reflects his strength and weakness in terms of achievements and possibilities on what could be achieved both in the present and in the future.

After listening to my inspirational teacher, I became more careful in many aspects of life as a whole. I began to learn from others, both near and far, and I began to have more value for my fellow humans by treating them with respect. I now value my time by being focus and determined towards whatever I want to achieve because I vividly remember the words uttered by that inspirational teacher.

Back to the story of the two grass cutters, one man later ended up with regret at night because the wise man later made a fortune, and because the second man carelessly lost the same opportunity by not being realistic about doing the right thing at the right time. The ability to make the right decisions in light of little or no resources in order to get the job done, reflects how effective a leader is.

So likewise, leaders would be judged by their performance and ability to successfully execute operational strategies to ensure organisational achievements. A story in one of the popular business magazines tells of a disappointed candidate who dreamed of succeeding the retiring chief executive officer at a well-known tobacco company, having served the organisation for twenty years, and rising to the position of director of operations after starting as a part time technical assistant. However, he was shut out after a middle manager made a petitioned against him, blaming his bad attitude and autocratic measures when coordinating team members (imposing his decisions and ideals on others regardless of the situation).

The director is well known for pretending to give the team members the chance to express their emotions and would always explain situations in an in-depth way, but made decisions based on a helicopter view, claiming that none of the team members knew or understood better than any of the board members. He later went as far as telling the same middle manager that regardless of knowledge, experience, and educational qualifications, he (the director) was still in charge of the team, and if the middle manager was interested in taking over, he should let him know. However, the director announced that he owned the final decision regarding the team. The young and aspiring middle manager felt humiliated in the presence of his colleagues, having been brought down in broad daylight by his senior colleague. After bringing this issue to light, the aspiring candidate began to warn other managers to stay clear of the middle manager, and began to frustrate him by assigning him difficult tasks with shorter deadlines, harshly imposing this attitude as the new culture. He later recommended to the board that every manager should reapply for his or her position due to high levels of ineffectiveness.

Meanwhile, the chief executive officer knew of the director's plans to get rid of the young manager, who had petitioned him either by dismissal or demotion. Unbeknownst to the director, the chief executive officer had brought the matter to the attention of other board members and advised them not to support him but to allow his one-horse race, knowing he had been given the go-ahead to conduct the interviews for middle line managers. At the end of the exercise, the director recommended that the young manger, whom he had never loved, be demoted with a significant possibility of dismissal. The middle manager began to apply for better opportunities outside the company the moment the restructuring process was announced because he could foresee what the future holds for him. A few days after the decision was made, the manager submitted his resignation letter to the chief executive officer, all to become a senior manager at a major competitor's organisation. What a huge blow to the organisation? The chief executive officer tried to sit the young manager to make known what the future of the organisation looks like, but "never a grace at a dead end", he replied and called it a day.

This made the chief executive officer sad, but it was too late to correct the situation by retaining the middle manager with some better promises for the future, so he smiled and wished him success for the future. In light of knowing his mistakes, shareholders began to mount pressure on the chief executive officer, having seen their competitor making serious waves in the market, forcing them to lose their position as market leaders, which they had held for years. Worst of all, the giant organisation began to experience a serious drop in its sales, which later became a major news headline on television. It became clear, however, that shareholders would experience a serious drop in their investment dividends.

At the next annual meeting, the chairman clearly stated that changing leadership would place the organisation in more trouble, but the chief executive officer should be given more time, with the target of adjusting the current situation, and also to nominate a successor, inasmuch as he had a year left prior to his retirement. Now the chief was left to identify the major cause of the problem, and seeking the best solution to the unexpected situation, he wisely employed the services of a highly-respected consulting firm to help find out the major parameters and platforms for their competitor's success.

However, at the end of the consultation, it was discovered that the former middle manager was the brain behind the success of the organisation, and facts revealed to the chief executive officer cleared the air—that the middle manager had a rapid promotion at the competitors' organisation due to his high level of experience.

The chief executive officer later came across a business magazine, in which the former manager was granted an interview. In it, he said that for leaders to be highly effective, they need to learn from their team members, and never dominate their team members to earn the best of their ideals, which would increase their knowledge about what to do at any particular time. While thinking of what to do, he was informed that the director, who was interested in his position upon his retirement, had begun to speak to the chairman and other key figures regarding his ambition. In light of this information, he then informed the board of his early retirement, and said he preferred the vacancy be advertised publicly so as to get the best candidate. The board embraced his ideal, and invited some other candidates to apply while the process was on-going.

The chairman and the board called a short meeting to find out why the chief executive officer couldn't recommend the director, who had a long service record, because it was believed that this director was the most suitable person for the job, and could hit the ground while running. This made the outgoing chief executive officer hammer the point home that he regretted not retaining the middle manager at the right time, since the aspiring director played ball right into the hands of their competitors. This happened as a result of his harsh leadership style and politics toward the middle manager, whom he frustrated due to his selfish interests. He also fired other managers who would have never bowed down to his toes, which made the organisation run out of operational and technical ideas when needed. The same manager later became the brain behind the strongest competitor the organisation ever had, making it lose its leadership with the industry it dominated as a result of his actions. The chairman could not fight his own cause, since he also experienced a drop in his dividends, and later made his concession, claiming it was a result of his inability to coordinate his team in the expected direction, and that he could not find effective support in any aspect related to his role as a director.

Another director later came along with an idea of inviting the former manager to apply for the role, since he was the major brain behind their competitor's success, and also knew how they operated. This would give them two major advantages for the organisation, giving him an edge over the aspiring director, and this situation left the aspiring director disappointed and sick for a while. He could not stand working under the former manager, and later left the organisation on confirmation of the former manager's appointment as the new chief executive.

Having read the story twice, I discovered a lot lessons to learn that could serve as a guide in one's career as a leader. For example, judgment came years after frustrating the middle manager out of the organisation, and when his performance was shown to the chairman, board of directors and other key stakeholders, his performance was less than expected. However, I could image how painful the experience must have been.

So likewise, leaders need to be very mindful of their relationship with their team members because the team members' achievements reflect the leader's credibility and capability which can work for or against them in any situation. Learning more lessons from the previous story, leaders need to create an environment which fosters high-performance which can be only achieved by creating value for the ideas of others. This serves as the brainpower within a work team, which can result in innovative products, services, and markets being unleashed.

It would be wise for all leaders to learn and adapt themselves to processes that could encourage the flow of ideas and solve complex problems. However, this would enable the understanding of behaviours which can accelerate high-performance via positive attributes within the work environment. Only if the careless farmer had made use of his friend's idea, he wouldn't have missed it all, and only if the director had been transparent to new ideas, he wouldn't have been seen as less effective to the organisation as a whole by the chairman at the point of achieving his aspirations after having served for years.

Becoming a high-performance leader doesn't occur by magic, but requires being effective at what needs to be done, knowing when to act, and how to get things done at various levels within the organisation. High performance in leadership is a step-by-step process that requires thought, discipline, and lots of hard work. The more focused and realistic a leader is about what needs to be done, the more likely he is to mount heights in his leadership career. The fewer excuses one gives, the more chances one has to be successful in anything one does.

Having risen to the strategic level within the third sector, coordinating and relating with various groups and stakeholders, I discovered that one of those things that makes and keeps a leader highly effective, is the ability to inspire those they lead. This is because it enables them to gain insight as to what the leader is trying to do when faced with increased complexity and uncertain situations. Inspiration would enable team members to look through the lens with a trained eye and see the possibility in what seems not to be possible. One major lesson from the story of the disappointed director is that leaders need to listen to their team members, regardless of the situation. I came to realize that some of the suggestions, information, and advice being passed on by the core operational staff are more useful for decision-making and strategic planning because the core operational staffs are properly tempered just like swords that are ready for battle. However, managers and executives only depend on the collected raw facts and figures presented as information by the tactical and operational staff for strategic planning and decision making.

Another point is the ability to listen, which gives leaders a better chance to influence their team members to gain their commitment toward what needs to be achieved within a certain period, which is a better way to make an effective impact in the development of individual team members. It's very important for any leader or executive to recognize, embrace, and apply the characteristics of high-performing terms in most successful organisations, which includes both the leader and team members having an agreed-upon mission or purpose in mind. These characteristics require leaders to be participative, which enables them to be seen as good role models, and also represents another way of gaining the commitment of others, making them believe that the leader knows and understands what their experiences are like. It creates an image of the leader as being democratic and not autocratic, and someone who has gotten a "we can win" thought pattern.

A participative leader respects the views of others by including them in the decision-making process where required, which is another characteristic of highly effective and performing teams, because it helps management gather accurate and relevant information for strategic framework and decision-making processes, which are aimed at remaining market leaders. However, including team members in the decision-making process reflects that they are being recognized and valued as stakeholders in their contributed efforts towards organisational success, which goes miles in creating an improved communication system within the organisation, and represents an essential tool for increasing trust, decreasing problems and conflict, and building healthy interpersonal relationships among team members. Leaders need to understand and recognize the beauty of having various kinds of people in a team, mostly from different backgrounds. This enhances diversity in thinking, ideas, methods, experiences, and opinions, which help in creating high-performance teams within an organisation.

In maintaining a highly effective and performing team, it's impossible to avoid have conflict among the team, which can become a serious challenge in handling it in the interest of team progress; otherwise, whatever affects the eye, affects the nose. However, conflict arises as a result of differences in personalities, beliefs and cultural background. In most cases, it is caused by misunderstanding in terms of communication, use of power, and values. As a matter of fact, it is paramount for leaders to familiarize themselves with updated and reasonable conflict-solving techniques, which requires training team members in conflict resolution to prevent or minimize potential conflicts.

In a nutshell, members of a high-performance team need to be given the freedom of expression, i.e., feeling free to share their concerns with others within an organisation without being seen as odd. In a nutshell, an effective leader needs to be approachable by ensuring team members of their contribution towards organisational growth will be appreciated. Team members need to be aware of the impact of a coordinated relationship, because each member is in need of the skills, knowledge, and expertise of all the other members to produce an expected and reliable result, because it remains the major pillar and purpose for accomplishing high-performance leadership within an organisation.

A tree can't make up a forest, as my former principal says. It's easier, more convenient, and reasonable to achieve success as a team rather than alone. As a matter of fact, a leader needs to surround himself or herself with like-minded people to keep them in the right place for success. There is always a sense of belonging, and a willingness to make things work in order to better the team when leaders listen to others and create a positive work and team atmosphere. In addition to these characteristics, leaders need to create plans to eradicate barriers to high-performance in every business unit of the organisation, and to learn from other organisations by forming alliances to effect positive change within the organisation. Effective leadership simply means surrounding oneself with people who have the right skills and competence to execute strategies effectively, which is a good platform in identifying and nurturing high-performance behaviours and teams throughout the organisation. The system of being highly effective requires leaders to develop a structured approach in preparing and thinking with more complexity about negotiations, and influencing everyday situations. These are very important steps in improving the leader's ability to influence others, to collaborate with other teams, and improve their negotiation skills, which are major parameters in leading effectively and driving a strategic direction. This is another reason why leaders need to be and remain highly effective, in order to possess the ability to leverage one's strengths in developing a strategic framework for avoiding negotiation traps while entering into agreement with other organisations, and also for improving teamwork.

Developing a relevant action plan in applying concepts and processes would enable leaders to identify bottlenecks and potential problems in operational processes, either personal or technical. The major purpose of building and maintaining high performing teams is to manage change effectively, and to adapt operational improvements in driving financial results and innovation, which is a major requirement in maintaining a better position within an industry.

Having attended an interactive discussion forum at an executive class, I learned that the fastest and most effective way to achieve profitable growth is for an organisation to focus on increasing the performance of its best team members. Even the highest-performing business units should be encouraged, and given the capacity to do better. In addition, team members falling behind should be assisted by giving the necessary support to help them improve.

Leaders need to optimize critical thinking within the team, and replicate high-performance practices throughout the organisation to achieve sustainable growth, and to identify ways to remove barriers that hinder performance. This includes dealing with highly politicized situations such as conflict of interest among team members.

Over the years, as a business coach, I have discovered the major reason why some leaders are more effective than others. This reason is that the ability to focus and execute basic strategic parameters to achieve the desired goal, varies among leaders. As I coach various clients, I do make it clear that the ability to learn and practise are major platforms to excellence.

Excellence in teamwork is the end product of effective

cooperation and dynamics within a particular team, which plays a huge role in enabling an organisation to function effectively. To achieve service excellence collectively as a team, it is important for leaders to build skills that can propel a team to move forward, share common goals, and have a strong internal customer, operational focus, and also understand the need to work together as a team, which is the reward when excellent service has been delivered.

Taking the constructive approach would enable leaders to see what their options and resources are. Making use of these resources quickly would also enable them to attain excellence alongside personal attributes such as courage, which would make it easier for both leaders and team members to conquer their fears and adversities. Courage makes it possible for one to maintain a comfortable state while facing an unpleasant situation, and enables one to carry on. However, courage does help leaders focus more on achieving a better result down the road, and remain realistic in whatever they are doing. Most times, in a leader's career, obstacles in the form of organisational policies and state laws do make it difficult to attain success in meeting their customers' and clients' needs. In reality, the quality and price of products and services are always determined by two major factors, i.e., local legislation and internal organisational politics. These make leaders face the huge challenge of maintaining the required standard expected of an organisational product or service, as well as making the forecasted profit so as to retain his job and make all stakeholders happy.

As I mentioned before during a coaching sessions few years ago, leaders should never regard a situation as being impossible. Instead, they should seek ways of constructively criticizing the local legislation which stands as a major obstacle, in the press, or in the form of interviews or articles, in which the legislation can be challenged for change. In most cases, it's better to state the negative impact of such legislation, such as the increase of unemployment, or a low standard in services, which is a better way to attract public awareness to force local legislators to make improvements regarding the situation. In some cases, it will require some form of dialogue. Another way of handing unpleasant situations is for leaders to ask other parties or stakeholders who are also affected, or have been affected by similar situations, what they did to handle such a problem. It's never the best thing for courageous leaders to hide behind policymaking as the reason for their failure. Facing the challenge of internal policies, leaders have a huge responsibility in making stakeholders understand the need for change in certain organisational cultures and what the positive impact of the intended change will be. The strength of a courageous leader can never be underestimated because courage is a great virtue that makes all other virtues in a leader possible and realistic.

In some situations, when all hope seems to be lost, while others see a dead end ahead, and see no meaning in what the leader is planning or executing, courage can and will enable others to see the meaning which was hidden from them right at the point they lost the insight required to see the big picture. Being courageous is not a matter of getting things done by force, although trying, failing, and improving are the major steps a courageous leader mounts during tough times towards success. I remember former British Prime Minister, James Gordon Brown, speaking at the Annual Labour Conference in 2008. He said; *tough times never weaken the determination of those who know what they are doing; rather, they strengthen their results.*

Later on, during his speech, I discovered how far courage could carry a man, both in his private life and career. One major fact every leader needs to know and understand is that obstacles and tough times are inevitable, and they only keep on highlighting the weaknesses you currently have, giving you reasons to give up, and magnifying "flaws" that block you from moving on. A courageous leader sees those situations as crabs in the bucket, disallowing others to mount up and move out of the bucket. He'd rather push harder to break out of the vacuum of limitation, and step up to the plate.

Confidence is another approach in boosting the strength and ability of a leader; it plays a huge role in bringing others along, because it's the cornerstone of leadership. Confidence requires leaders to believe in themselves, because without it, it's impossible to be an effective problem solver, effective decision maker, and a better communicator. As Francisco Dao, the founder of 50 Kings said, *"Self-confidence is the fundamental basis from which leadership grows. Trying to lead others without first building confidence is like building a house without a solid foundation. It may have a nice coat of paint, but it is ultimately shaky at best."* However, confidence in leaders makes them motivated and ambitious, which enables them to set goals, and parameters to accomplish them. They prefer to create better and strategic relationships by entering into positive and productive relationships. They believe in win-win outcomes and don't think of keeping the whole pie for themselves. Confidence enables leaders to remain open in recognizing success when achieved not only by themselves, but by others, and they constantly seek ways for improvement; they welcome feedback from others, and put their ideas into action at various points in time. Without confidence, a project could end up failing. Leaders need to bear in mind that self-confidence is indeed a very important component of their leadership role, and often pays better than any financial reward.

Leadership without respect is meaningless. For a leader to command a good level of respect, such leader needs to be disciplined. In a nutshell, a lot of writers and authors refer to this as self-discipline, which is the ability to get oneself to take an action regardless of one's emotional state, whether favourable or unfavourable. My mother once told me when I was young that discipline is the ability of a man to execute correct judgment all the time. According to Author H. Jackson Brown Jr., *"Talent without discipline is like an octopus on roller skates. There's plenty of movement, but you never know if it's going to be forward, backwards, or sideways."* In other words, no matter how perfect a leader might be, it takes discipline to maintain a good level of focus and direction, and to attain greater heights in one's career. If discipline is lacking in leadership, it's difficult to lead others. In an ever-changing and globalized world, leaders are often faced with high expectations which require them to be self-disciplined and knowledgeable, so as to make the right judgment at any given time in the realistic allocation of organisational resources.

A friend of mine told me a story about her boss, who was jailed for lack of discipline in one of the local councils in the United Kingdom some years ago. He was the head of the department for highways and technical services, in which one of the major functions was to repair and maintain all roads within the borough. When the current road maintenance contract was running out, the contract manager made a phone call regarding its renewal, requesting an increase due to inflation, and some other overhead costs. The head of the department decided to make a request for an out-of-office call on his private mobile phone. The contract manager smelled a rat, and suspected that something unethical was about to take place. What the HOD never knew was that he was being filmed telling the contract manager he was ready to award the contract to a friend, but would like to know what the company could give him in return. The contract manager wisely told him that the director would have the final say in the decision, to which the HOD agreed. Later, the director called the HOD, who asked for 15,000 pounds. When the director requested his bank details, the HOD foolishly gave two different account details in order to share the money. Unknown to him, the person he gave his account details to was a police officer. A few days later, he called the contract manger and said that he is awaiting the money transfer to his account, without knowing there were other on-going investigations regarding his on-the-job business activities. A number of irregularities were discovered, which later got him arrested. To cut the story short, he was jailed for 37 months. He was a promising young man, age 42, who wasted his future as a result of a lack of discipline.

In fact, discipline is an important quality for anyone aspiring to greatness, and is always required when in a leadership position. Discipline facilitates trust, which enables stakeholders to believe in a leader's ability, because it reflects what a leader stands for. There is no beating round the bush; *trust is a must for anyone to become an effective, high-performance leader.* One must earn the trust and confidence of others to enable everyone to operate successfully.

Otherwise, doubts about one's ability frustrate people, and cause them to lose focus and end up missing target goals. Knowing the importance of trust, once it is established, it's advisable for one to keep it, maintain it, and guard it, because it's a valuable virtue in leadership as a whole, and it shouldn't be taken for granted. As I once told a client of mine, who happens to be a senior manager in a third sector organisation, trust cannot be forced on stakeholders. Rather, a leader needs to earn it, and once earned, it should be cherished, because once lost, it could take a lifetime to regain.

Maturity is another aspect in leaders that one needs to take seriously, because it enables leaders to deal with issues in the most accepted manner. It grants a leader the ability to focus on both results and relationships required to achieve a sustainable level of high-performance. Maturity is an end-product of development, and helps leaders in terms of growth in all other aspects, such as the ability to take initiative, which reflects how ambitious and innovative a leader is. Maturity also shows how the ability to take initiative creates and inspires leaders to take action and make things happen. However, a vision without action is just a dream, so, likewise, it requires maturity to take the right step, at the right place, at the right time, as to make a vision a reality, because without initiative, ideas go nowhere.

Emotional intelligence is another area of leadership. Leaders need emotional intelligence because it enables them to understand and manage their emotions and those of others around them. Emotional intelligence also provides leaders with other skills, such as the ability to manage relationships, navigate social networks, to influence and inspire others. It's about understanding one's self and others for a common purpose. A major need for emotional intelligence within an organisation is because of its impact in conflict resolution, which aims to deal with unpleasant situations which can threaten or disrupt efficiency and productivity. With this skill, leaders can quickly placate any disagreements that arise between stakeholders. Maturity enables a leader to be patient, mostly when facing difficulties in their relationships with others, when a situation requires a change with different stages which might take time for people to adapt. Patience carries a leader a long way in relating, managing, and leading people. An African proverb says: *"with time, an egg would walk"*. Another one says: *"a quiet dog eats the fattest bone"*. Life is never a bed of roses; some days are good, and some are bad. Whenever a leader is passing through tough times, it's good to persevere. Perseverance is a quality of a good leader because it reflects how strong and durable one is in spite of difficulties, obstacles or whatever discouragement he or she faces. According to a friend of mine, a motivational speaker, Beatrice Majekodunmi once said: *"a great leader would examine the circumstances in any difficult situation and find a potential solution, along with a set of tools and methods to allow the organisation to persevere through the obstacle and continue on the road to successfully achieving their goals."*

Another benefit of maturity in leadership is that it enables leaders to focus and stick to the major purpose the organisation was formed to achieve, be it profit or not. Sticking to purpose plays a huge role in the daily running of an organisation, and also in areas of accountability. Sticking to the core purpose of an organisation enables it to focus more on its desired direction and other reasonable parameters. Some of these parameters are: Where are we going? How do we get there? Sticking to what an organisation stands for, and getting every stakeholder on board, enables a leader stay on course.

However, the strength of leaders is the ability to face down tough times and face constant change and challenges with limited resources and perfect execution. It's not sufficient and reasonable for a leader to settle and dwell within his or her comfort zone and just believe in surviving and remaining stagnant. Going the extra mile is an example of thriving, which enables leaders to make steady progress, grow vigorously, and flourish in their field. Never should any leader or manager lead others while depending solely on his or her previous knowledge or experience, because the world changes on a continuous basis, so therefore, it requires leaders to update their knowledge and skills to make them current with any changes.

CHAPTER 2

THE NEED FOR HIGH-
PERFORMANCE LEADERSHIP

The strength of a leader is the ability to deliver high-level expertise at strategic and corporate levels, which is in line with high-performance leadership, and is required in helping organisations transform and develop leaders who are able to master the challenges of a complex and changing world. For a leader's strength to be meaningful, his knowledge on leadership development has to be ascertained at three different levels to drive organisational success. This includes identifying, formulating, and executing strategies alongside with other leadership qualities.

However, identifying strategies for an organisation is not a matter of guesswork or adapting a competitor's strategy simply because it worked for that entity. Leaders need to identify a reasonable and applicable strategy which is in line with helping an organisation achieve its major objectives, regardless of challenges and barriers. The act of identifying strategies for an organisation plays a huge role in planning its future. This includes a leader's ability to know and understand his industry, stakeholders, and customers. It requires the ability for leaders to analyse current situations facing their organisation, and examining long- term goals and other key areas which are of critical importance to their organisation. Assessing the viability of one's idea is another element to be evaluated when identifying strategies for an organisation. The continuous need for growth is another key element to be considered when adapting strategies in terms of evaluating competitors.

Strategy formulation, which is the process of establishing an organisation's mission and objectives, occurs as a result of selecting from alternative strategies for implementation. Some authors and researchers refer to strategy formulation as strategic planning. Strategy formulation deals with how to design an organisational implementation process and assess any weaknesses in the selected implementation plan. Then, strategy is translated into action by getting the right people on board to get the job done, assessing potential resistance to change, and seeking preventive measures on how best to manage, approach, and deal with risk.

I do see strategy execution as the act of getting things done, which involves a step-by-step process. However, strategy execution is essential in driving results. In other words, strategic execution could be classified as the combination of a leader's capability, i.e., having the right skills and knowledge to make the right decisions for organisational transformation. The leader's mind-set, i.e., believing in oneself, must be capable to lead others without any form of doubt or fear. Leaders must know what they want to do, and how best to do it. The strategic alignment of an organisation as a whole signifies the intended direction of an organisation, i.e., where to go, why, and how to get there, which are the major cornerstones of an organisation's foundation, which all other aspects rest on.

Strategic alignment does reflect where an organisation stands among others within the same industry. Having made an overview of strategic execution, which I refer to as a step-by-step process, let's bear in mind that one cap doesn't fit all. The steps might be applicable in some organisations, but not in others. The five steps outlined below have been proven by various consultants across the globe, due to their ability in helping both leaders and their organisations to provide perfect direction.

Step 1: Visualizing the strategy. This is one of the most pressing challenges in all forms of strategy, which requires leaders to have the ability to simplify and understand what a strategy is. The process of visualizing a strategy enables leaders have an idea of the potential impact of the intended strategy. An effective way to visualize strategies is usually via the use of illustrations, or a framework which shows both the important elements of the strategy and how each relates to the current need of the organisation. An example of such a framework includes the Activity Map by Michael Porter.

Step 2: Measuring the strategy based on what it requires in terms of transformation. This is a key element in any selected strategy in terms of performance measures which all stakeholders of an organisation need to understand. The performance measurement serves as yardstick in terms of what is expected at regular intervals in the implementation of a strategy. Common strategic performance measurement tools are the Balanced Scorecard and the key performance indicator.

Step 3: Making clear decisions. Strategy execution is much like sailing a boat towards a planned destination. A leader's act in making clear decisions needs to pass the fundamental test of an organisation: Where are we now? Where do we want to be? How do we get there? The same act enables leaders to map out roles and responsibilities for execution along with a deadline. Leaders should never be afraid of making decision while also taking steps; it's a good way of building one's confidence.

Step 4: Aligning strategy with goals. Once a course of action has been defined, leaders need to align the strategy with the required process to attain organisational goals. This process would enable leaders to increase their operating margins by communicating expectations clearly during every phase of goal completion, increasing employee engagement, and by creating shared accountability between employees. To align strategies with overall organisational goals, leaders need to embrace strategic thinking processes.

Step 5: Reward performance. In strategy execution, as in any other area of management, what gets measured, gets done. Taking this one step further, what gets measured and rewarded, gets done faster. After explaining the strategy and aligning the workforce to it, senior managers institute the incentives that drive behaviours consistent with the strategy. However, a reasonable reward system needs to include locally competitive rewards within an industrial framework, and also needs to be differentiated in terms of attracting and retaining skilled employees.

The above is easier said than done. Strategy execution is difficult in practice for many reasons, but a key impediment to success is that many leaders don't know what strategy execution is, or how they should approach it.

The strength of a leader enables him or her to develop and implement transformational leadership and succession-planning initiatives through one-on-one executive coaching and other related seminars.

Another important indicator of adequate strength in a leader is that he serves as a platform for high-performance leadership in maintaining a good position within the industry, which is a competitive advantage in the global marketplace. In terms of positioning for competitive advantages, I usually tell my clients; *that where you stand determines who sees you, and who sees you determines what you get or achieve, and you achieve determines what you can establish within any given state.*

Leaders need to be consistent to gain the trust and the confidence of their clients and other stakeholders which serve as a boost to their ability and qualities. Consistency requires leaders to approach matters similarly and not robbing Paul to pay Peter. Effective leadership involves moving others toward a shared and defined vision that results in accomplished goals, which are the end-product of high-performance leadership. As I was told by a lecturer of mine at a postgraduate class, accepted success lies in the ability of a leader to be able to make stakeholders have a clear understanding of the mission and vision of their organisation, along with the strategies to achieve them. However, I still remember how the lecturer went on to explain the importance of team building, quality improvement, and problem solving, which all involves leaders engaging and empowering others in processes and systems required in attaining organisational success. As I usually say, a tree doesn't make a forest, which means that a leader requires the joint effort of others to achieve palpable results.

Being an effective leader desiring high-performance requires the ability to listen and inspire, as well as being able to compel the team toward the organisational vision. Leaders need the confidence and emotional intelligence required to relate to others, and also the sense to take risks when necessary. A leader's strength can be demonstrated at three different stages: at the personal level, at the team level, and at the organisational level.

The personal level is a stage whereby leaders perform and execute based on their personal character and beliefs, which become critical factors in their relationships with others within the organisation. Another aspect at this level is that most leaders see their style as a platform for their growth and development, which enables them to clarify their personal purpose and vision. Leaders need to understand more about interacting with others and developing the awareness and personal maturity in making right choices and decisions. Leaders who believe in this style are often seen as role models because they are known to have been inspired by helping others build their confidence, and enabling them to retain focus and commitment, which are required elements to help them achieve better results within a certain period. It would be clever of leaders to review their experiences and performance while relating to others, mostly in areas such as outcomes and feedback, and learn from every situation for continuous improvement.

However, at the team level, leaders become more accountable for their actions and the performance of others on their teams. The major challenge remains the ability of leaders to be equipped with the required wisdom and skills to create an environment that makes others fully engaged and effective in fulfilling the mission of the organisation.

However, at the team level, leaders have to strive for competitiveness in terms of attaining high-performance on the part of team members. This remains critical to organisational success, due to the huge responsibility of the leader. The leader is responsible for developing and utilising a diverse team of people with different strengths and skills who are closely aligned with crucial business functions at various sectors within the organisation. All team members are responsible for generating, maintaining, and focusing on the team purpose, as well as setting explicit goals. The leader's job is building strong relationships with team members to capitalise on their strengths and stimulate continuous improvement for better results. However, more is expected of a leader at the team stage, in terms of establishing a focused communication process, and regular performance reviews, which serve as a control geared towards attaining the desired result. It's also paramount for leaders to recognise every key milestone attained, and celebrate success. According to John Maxwell, in his book, *Leadership Gold,* in order for leaders to get the best of their team's strength, they should never send their ducks to eagle school. In my own view, for leaders to lead members towards success, there is a huge need to identify and recognize their individual talents and skills to know where best to place them in terms of strategic execution. Similar to a football term, the coach knows which wing to place each player in line with their capability, which creates a better platform for expectation.

The last stage is the organisational level, which is all about productivity. The major factor at this stage is the leader's ability to be and remain effective at taking a holistic view of the organisation's performance, and plan interventions that define direction, create infrastructure, and promote a positive culture. The key elements at this stage include the expected of level of performance to be achieved at various times. The competencies needed to achieve this level of performance are mostly at the strategic level, due to the sensitivity required here. This is because a failure in one area can cause a failure in all operational systems of an organisation. So it's important to motivate and empower team members, to monitor and review those mechanisms which measure their performance, and compare results with actual targets alongside with the required measures needed to improve performance so as to attain best practices. However, a leader needs to bear in mind that all measures taken to ensure the planned targets and competencies should be the best options at any given time, to the best of their knowledge, skills and abilities, and also in the best interests of all stakeholders.

The truth about a leader's strength is the ability of any leader to face and handle the business environment challenges in attaining and remaining industry leaders by placing major consideration on the following parameters: what needs to be done, how it can be done, and how the business can maintain its position within the industry.

Another point about the leader's strength is that it enhances high-performance within an organisation because it enables the leader to put in motion reasonable sets of criteria, such as ensuring that employees' goals are aligned with those of the organisation, and establishing priorities for both the organisation and the employees that reflect the business and its organisational demands. The business goals and criteria also assume exceptional performance standards, achieved over time, and under pressure. However, a reasonable goal needs to possess the element of possibility in terms of attaining it.

I remember my former tutor, Dr Abraham Adefenwa, once said at a strategic management class held in London, that it was important for organisations and their leaders to invest more in initiatives to develop team skills and attitudes which would promote healthy team dynamics. This, he said, would help them remain highly productive by increasing quality, reducing overhead costs where necessary, and being accurate in meeting demand.

From my experience as an executive coach, I advise managers, team leaders, and other strategic position officers to ensure they work hard to understand the predictable steps which enhance team performance, and also to always seek common ground to facilitate good communication among team members. These are major characteristics that consistently achieve exceptional results for an organisation as a whole. In addition, there are needs for internal measures, which help in building the inner systems and processes of the team which are facilitated as a result of better understanding. These include control, which is an operational function of supervising and supporting each other, mostly in a multitasking and pressure situation, which in most cases requires a joint effort to produce results in a friendly and honest manner, without confrontation or blame regarding unexpected performance. Teams should seek alternative methods for improvement and give support where needed at the right time.

Trust is another internal and vital measure in which every team needs to lay its foundation, because trust displaces self-centeredness, which could inject mistrust among team members. However, trust is a pillar which continuously enables leaders and team members to gain mutual interest by eliminating conflicts of interest. Trust is a serious parameter in ensuring the smooth running of operations and delivering service. No leader can force trust on others. Trust can only be earned. It also enables two leaders and their members to be honest towards each other. One thing I do hammer home is that leaders should always give team members the benefit of the doubt, regardless of the situation. This is a platform for leaders to establish trust within a team that includes the ability and capability for them to strive and ensure that they perform their expected duties and obligations competently, without depending too much on team members. This helps them maintain a high level of consistency in terms of their behaviours and predictable patterns in getting things done. However, leaders should endeavour to respect the concerns of others, and their commitment towards the success of their organisation as whole. Leaders need to share and delegate control to reflect transparency.

Involvement is a unique method of increasing team and organisational flexibility, efficiency and productivity. However, involvement increases the interest and willingness for both leaders and team members to develop a long-term relationship with an organisation, and in its activities in ensuring its desired achievement. As part of a leader's function, it's advisable to build a collaborative team and work environment, aiming for a common goal. In a nutshell, the involvement of team members is very vital to both operational and organisational success. Just as a tree would never make a forest, so likewise a leader would never achieve it all alone without the effort of others.

Coordination creates a platform for improvement, because its function is more one of ensuring that every single effort in an operational process is in perfect order toward an improved joint performance. Leaders need to be very assertive in seeing that every team member is meeting their individual targets, because they face the music all alone when the output is below expectation. As a matter of fact, the major role of coordination is to ensure the clarification of roles by making sure that everyone knows his or her role, and is familiar with their expectations and responsibilities. However, roles, expectations and responsibilities need to be creative, realistic, and also have an impact on both the team and organisational operational processes, in terms of execution to enhance efficiency and flexibility. However, it is also a better practice for managers and leaders at all levels within an organisation to review their team members' roles frequently, relate their team members' individual expectations and performance to the team's overall common purpose. Reviewing team performance is a better way of learning more about the impact of each member on the overall team success of the organisation, and also figuring out ways to help each other—especially the new and inexperienced members. The impact of every little grain of salt added goes a long way to determine the taste of soup, *an African proverb*, and without the last brick, the building remains incomplete, so therefore, leaders need to cherish every little contribution made by their team members toward achieving overall success.

Dependence. Mutual dependency occurs when both parties invest an equal amount of time and money in a relationship. Communication in any organisation needs to be taken seriously and made paramount so as to give organisational strategies great meaning, while presenting them to stakeholders in order to reduce fear and doubt in their investment and involvement in the organisation. Communication needs to be continuous to remain effective, to ensure that all parties are informed and updated at regular intervals about any changes in policy, innovation, and management within an organisation. In a realistic mode of communication, it's up to the leader to bear the responsibility of ensuring that stakeholders are being heard and understood at any point in time.

Diversity is another major part of a team's inner system, because it requires recognizing and appreciating the uniqueness of the other members. Having respect for diversity is for every team member, including the leader, to see that everyone is equal, and not seeing themselves as being too relevant at the expense of becoming irrelevant later in the day. Leaders need to understand that team members are made up individuals who come from all walks of life. They have different backgrounds and perspectives, different cultures, thinking and beliefs, in which the timely challenge requires the ability to accept and cope with each other, regardless of differences, to work for a common purpose in a conductive environment. This is a better way of reflecting and promoting diversity.

On the other hand, team members need to recognize the impact of their various expectations in terms of their performance measures, and the impact on the overall team's output. They shouldn't they see monitoring as means of punishment, but rather as a platform for the improvement of their skills and attributes, which are essential for the team's internal group dynamics and relationships. Both managers and leaders are expected to regularly review and evaluate the effectiveness of their members by designing an individual's performance reflector in relationship to the expected goals, in tabulated form at team meetings, to identify causes of interruption and other bottlenecks affecting the team operations, and also by discussing possible ways for improvement.

As mentioned earlier in this book, leaders need to recognize the importance of celebrating achievement, which motivates team members to be more committed by putting in more effort toward achieving more results at later periods. However, at the point of identifying causes responsible for weaknesses, it's wiser for a leader to share the tougher tasks among members, mostly making new or inexperienced members learn from the experienced ones, which is a good avenue for leaders to monitor both tasks and relationship needs.

CHAPTER 3

PILLARS FOR HIGH-PERFORMANCE LEADERSHIP

The ability to successfully execute ideas and strategies is what separates the dreamers from visionaries, and makes them great leaders. It requires action for leaders to reflect their personality. Effective leadership requires intuition. This is true mostly when leading an organisation through uncharted waters, when the future seems to be dark, and organisational stakeholders wish to know and understand the intended line of action and direction the organisation would likely take to avoid losses and wastage. It's the major responsibility of leaders to clear the air at any point in time. Learning from both one's and others' previous experiences facilitates a good level of confidence and competence to enable others within an organisation to trust them in moving the organisation forward, regardless of what they face.

However, the first pillar every leader needs to hold onto is courage. According to John Maxwell, in his book, 21 Indispensable Qualities of a Leader, *one with courage is a majority.* Courage enables one to carry on regardless of the number of trials and obstacles in both private and social life. However, I see the pillars for high-performance leadership as the personal attitudes leaders need to establish within an organisation, which include the following.

HONESTY

Leaders need to lend themselves to credibility in order to make a positive reflection as to what they stand for under any circumstance. Such leaders prefer obstacles to be addressed rather than avoided. They hit the nail on the head in light of any situation. Honesty can be seen as the ability to be and remain transparent and open to stakeholders, along with the willingness to communicate one's emotions to others, even when a situation is uncomfortable. Honesty can be seen as the willingness to listen and discuss vital organisational issues ahead of decision-making, i.e., revealing relevant facts and figures regarding a situation in a true and fair manner. Honesty as a whole is simply doing what's right in an accepted manner. In a nutshell, honesty could be referred to as the different aspects of moral character in a leader. It also indicates positive and virtuous attributes such as integrity, truthfulness, and straightforwardness, which are essential to a leader's legitimacy, credibility, and ability to develop trust among stakeholders.

ABILITY TO DELEGATE

Delegation is the on-going process by which a leader assigns additional tasks (i.e., legitimate authority and responsibility) to team members in which there is an acceptance of responsibility for the assigned tasks. Delegation speeds the rate of delivery in attaining a goal because the task is broken down into simpler and smaller units, which eases work pressures and increases time for meeting targets, due to the allocation of roles and responsibilities. The delegation process facilitates effectiveness within an operational system. However, delegation is a process that increases the rate of development and motivation of team members while facing more challenges. They generally see and take them as opportunities to learn, grow, and be more mature in handling more complex issues, and also boost their courage and confidence in taking on more duties.

This ability to delegate speeds up execution and the

encouragement for growth within an organisation. However, it creates a more productive environment, and enhances productivity levels. Delegation enables both leaders and subordinates to remain focused on what's important for the organisation in the long term, and not just the short run, i.e., by being strategic. Delegating as a whole encourages a team approach in doing and getting done by involving everyone in the success of the organisation. I do remember a friend of mine, a parking enforcement manager, who explained in brief what his job description includes: - maintaining parking assets in the most appropriate manner, ensuring proper methods and controls are maintained over all parking activities, ensuring compliance with all statutory and regulatory requirements, liaising with outside and national bodies, attend meetings often outside normal working hours. His job also includes managing the work of various teams and staff, reporting to the post holder to meet programme, financial, and performance targets and to ensure the effective use of staff and physical and financial resources to achieve the best value, developing and managing the performance of the teams and staff reporting to the post holder, ensuring that staff has access to the information, training and development that they need to discharge their duties effectively, improving the management of parking operations and enforcement to improve customer care, meeting quality standards, providing professional advice and expertise on operational parking matters based on up-to-date knowledge of the relevant legislation and up-to-date good practice, to Members, staff, public utilities, Government departments, other professionals, contractors, partners, and the wider community including businesses, developers and local residents and under legal cross-examination as required, so as to ensure that the organis-ational objectives are effectively achieved. So, what's the magic behind your success? I asked. I do delegate some roles to my deputy managers who later share some basis roles with their respective officers. Some good reasons to delegate includes the impact it has on saving managerial time; it's a better way of developing employees by engaging and motivating them.

COMMUNICATION

Effective communication helps leaders keep teams working on the right projects with the right attitude. Once leaders communicate effectively about expectations, issues, and advice, stakeholders are likely to understand the leader's vision and goals.

Knowing what a leader wants to accomplish within a time frame makes it easier to communicate in terms of where to maintain focus and invest resources. Effective communication requires the right skill in order to be able to clarify and succinctly describe what a leader wants done, which is extremely important for the growth of the organisation, keeping its needs in line with the organisational vision and mission. Communication is extremely powerful; a lot has been said and written about it in terms of its role and impact.

SENSE OF HUMOUR

Leaders need to find a way to lighten up the atmosphere to carry others along without being bored. A good sense of humour fosters productivity, effective communication, and collaboration between stakeholders, and also creates a common ground in most negotiation processes. Leaders with a sense of humour are better equipped to handle unexpected crisis situations. A good sense of humour helps leaders earn respect, and maintain a good of integrity within and outside an organisation. Humour relieves tension during difficult times, and leaders with a sense of humour showcase positivity within an organisation.

COMMITMENT

According to Dr John Maxwell, in his book, *21 Indispensable Qualities of a Leader*, commitment separates the doers from the dreamers. It always requires a huge interest and hard work alongside commitment in both team and organisational activities to produce quality content. A committed leader always leads by example. However, commitment as a platform for motivating others must be dedicated to achieving success as an organisation. From experience, committed leaders and managers earn a lot of respect because others see them as going the extra mile in attaining success for the organisation. Apart from respect, commitment is about leaders knowing and fulfilling their obligations along with the willingness to sacrifice, which boosts their reputation and credibility as leaders. However, having the elements of credibility, a leader is more likely to deliver the peak amount of quality service possible.

Knowing and fulfilling one's obligations as a leader requires the ability to know what to do and how to do it at any given situation, because every leader has the duty to care for all stakeholders in one form or another. It's the leader's obligation to be effective, and remain certain of what is being done, and he should be able to stand by it. This is a major obligation of every set, to maintain a higher standard in terms of behaviour, and is another form of expectation from stakeholders. Leaders should always recognize their limitations in all they do. Another point mentioned above is the willingness to sacrifice, which reflects the conviction, commitment and competency of a leader in ensuring the success of an organis- ation, regardless of what it might it cost to achieve success. In most cases, it requires leaders to give up things that are of value in the short run for a long-term purpose, which is always of greater value.

POSITIVE ATTITUDE

This is what every leader needs to keep his team and other stakeholders motivated for the continued success of an organisation. It requires the leader to be realistic by making sure his goals are achievable. However, it's advisable for such leaders to associate with positive people, because *two heads are better than one*. My mother once told me it's better to maintain a positive attitude in the midst of uncertainties, because success follows a process, and not magic which can be gained at a spot. Positive attitudes attract creative thinking, which is a good pattern for growth, and is also essential in leading an organisation successfully.

ABILITY TO INSPIRE OTHERS

This is the ability to help people reach their potential in terms of peak performance via various form of support. The major purpose of an inspirational leader is to make a positive impact within the organisation, and to make success a reality, which requires leaders to be passionate, purpose driven, and have the ability to listen more, and talk less.

In my experience as a business coach, the ability to inspire others requires four major factors in leaders: (1) the ability to lead by example; (2) the ability to believe in the future; (3) the ability to connect with people via effective communication; (4) the ability to develop and help people to believe in themselves.

1) The ability to lead by example enables leaders to freely develop and support others in form of professional development to promote strategic cooperation within an organisation. Leading by example makes easier for leaders to manage around obstacles, defuse tension, manage crises and develop team confidence.

2) The ability to believe in the future requires leaders to believe in what they stand for, regardless of the challenges they face. According to Eleanor Roosevelt; *the future belongs to those who believe in the beauty of their dreams. Not just that, it requires leaders to work on their confidence as well.*

3) The ability to connect with people via effective communication; A lot has been said on that, yet it remains a powerful tool for moving an organisation forward.

4) The ability to develop and help people to believe in themselves. These are processes that includes, involving people in decision making, emphasising problem solving techniques to help develop knowledge and skills of team members.

A leader who is trusted and collaborates across an organisation is more impactful than a leader doing things for the sake of being paid. Another powerful point about inspiration is the ability to get things done rather than ditching it. This enables one to be an achiever rather than a dreamer.

ABILITY TO TURN AROUND WEAKNESSES

Weakness of attitude becomes weakness of character. ~ Albert Einstein

There is huge need for leaders to seek ways to improve their ability, or else it might pull them down in light of innovation and change. Seeking support from others and coaching are both good methods of managing one's weaknesses. However, it's important for leaders to acknowledge the need for improvement, which helps in designing the process for correction, or else efforts and resources could be rendered baseless. In managing weaknesses, it is wiser for leaders to delegate the tougher tasks to subordinates or outside contractors, and set quantifiable goals in terms of expectations. Leaders also need to learn how those activities are being done.

Taking insight from The Karate Kid movie released in 2010, which casted Jaden Smith as Dre Parker and Jackie Chan as Mr Han, one of the interesting lessons I learned from the movie was when all hope seemed to be lost for Dre Parker due to his struggling situation. This is where Mr Han kept on telling him to remain focused. I saw in this clever advice a platform for helping Dre Parker turn around his weakness by identifying the weak point of his counterpart, in which he later did and won the trophy, focusing more on his strengths and improving his abilities. This is what gave him the edge.

According to Oprah Winfrey, *"Where there is no struggle, there is no strength."*

This quote indicates that the struggle creates the need for strength. However, leaders should avoid pretending that all is well when it's not. A weakness has to be admitted to exist in a clear manner in order to indicate whether or not improvement is required.

I would personally explore upcoming leaders, and to seek advice and guidance from the elderly ones via reading their books, listening to tapes or audio books. With experienced leaders, this helps to a large extend in identifying blind spots affecting such leaders' growth. Assessing oneself regularly is another approach when dealing with weaknesses, because it reflects how good one is at some specific tasks alongside measures for continuous improvement.

However, in the simple context of it, continuous improvement should always remain an on-going concern effort in terms of improving organisational output, services or processes. Continuous improvement should be undertaken at regular intervals, as a result of embracing innovation and avoiding breakdowns in organisational operational processes.

A common and widely used tool for continuous improvement is a four-step quality model, i.e., the plan-do-check-act (PDCA) cycle:

Plan: Identify an opportunity and plan for change.

Do: Implement the change on a small scale.

Check: Use data to analyse the results of the change, and determine whether it made a difference.

Act: If the change was successful, implement it on a wider scale, and continuously assess your results. If the change did not work, begin the cycle again.

However, turning around one's weakness is a matter of continual trial leading to improvement, which should lay more emphasis on major organisational components such as leadership, communication, resources, organisation, architecture, people and processes. Once an organisation has identified its critical success factors, then it's time to focus on the continual improvement parameters of its processes and operations.

CHAPTER 4

FEATURES OF HIGH-PERFORMANCE TEAMS

Having studied and coached teams and teamwork over the years, I have consistently found similar qualities in teams that achieve exceptional results. I once studied four different teams within the same organisation, having coached their leaders and conducted a group coaching session for each team on the importance of mutual understanding within members. After a while, I noticed six common features a coach friend of mine tried, and got the same result. The first feature that makes a team highly effective in terms of performance is that those teams have, and stick to, a common purpose, which is the most important ingredient a team needs to achieve success on a clear ground of reality. This fact is a matter of no ifs, ands, or buts. The major importance of having a common purpose is to make members more committed to the team's objectives, which are always achievable through collaboration. Leaders need to understand the major key element of having a common purpose while leading others, which is essential for team alignment, because it enables teams of all types, at every level of the organisation, to rapidly accelerate performance.

Such key elements include the common purpose, which is: **Clear**, which makes it understood by all relevant stakeholders; **Relevant,** which enables leaders to align the team goals to individual interests; **Significant**, and this function makes the purpose worthwhile; **Achievable**, this makes everyone believe the team purpose is realistic and attainable; **Urgent**, which gives a sense of timeliness, which drives performance. However, the fact remains that if there's no common purpose, there's no team performance.

Another feature of high-performance teams is that they stick to clear roles, which serve as a parameter for apportioning different roles in relation to the collective work within a team. However, clarifying roles is about the designing, division, and deployment of the work to be done within a team. Leaders need to be realistic in clearing and apportioning roles, knowing each member's strengths and weaknesses.

As John Maxwell wrote in his book, *Leadership Gold*, never should a leader send his ducks to eagles school, stating the need of leaders to allocate roles within a team according to individual strengths. Having competent leadership is another serious parameter in attaining high performance within teams and organisations, because once the head is down, the whole body falls — a popular African proverb. In a nutshell any breakdown in an operational system is always being regarded as a result of ineffectiveness on the side of the leader. Therefore, where competent leadership is lacking, the whole team loses it all.

The purpose of competencies in leadership is their ability to provide and give better direction for an organisation, in which there is a need for effectiveness to attain a better direction. Building and maintaining an effective process is another essential parameter in attaining a better performance level within an organisation's various units. In the long run, it requires a high level of competencies in aligning team members and operations for reasonable results in terms of overcoming barriers and obstacles in operational processes. Processes are smaller units of any given operation, which are required for perfect execution. However, leaders need to employ the services of experienced members to handle various tasks at different stages to make the operation meaningful. Team members need to be friends; as a matter of fact, they need to maintain solid relationships along with effective communication, which makes it easier to work with each other by combining a diversity of skills, experience, and knowledge, which are needed to attain and maintain a high level performance. However, building and maintaining solid team relationships always provides the climate for high levels of collaboration, which later creates the need for trust, acceptance, respect, understanding, and courtesy.

In a nutshell, these characterisers are non-negotiable elements in building and maintaining solid relationships.

For an organisation to make its products and services known globally, it has to communicate both internally and externally. The internal aspect is how the leaders, directors, and managers decide to produce specific goods and services alongside with when and where to make them available at a specific time in the market, while the external aspect deals with adverting and publicity of those goods and services, via various mediums such as Internet, television, and billboards. In a nutshell, effective communication is a hallmark of high levels of team performance, which is essential for better results within an organisation.

Having explained the features of high-performance teams, there is also a need to explain the mistakes leaders make on a regular basis, which accounted for their failure. We all understand that there are expectations for every member of an organisation, yet no leader or manager can achieve 100 percent in terms of stakeholders' expectations with their performance. However, leaders minimizing their mistakes act as a stepping stone toward improvement, and avoids having them recur, such as not focusing on major priorities, which makes it easier for a leader or manager to find himself off the track, as Daniel Goleman refers to focus as the hidden driver of excellence. In the real sense of it, for a leader to be successful, there is a huge need for focus. I remember a student preparing for an exam who was listening to music at the same time. She sat in the examination hall writing down the lyrics of the music she was listening to while she was preparing for her exams, and later came to her senses, and had to cancel the nonsense she had wasted her time writing, when she had less time left to complete the exam. In other words, being focused on major priorities at the right time drives excellence, both in the long and short run because it enables leaders to utilize the best of their time and resources. Leaders should see leadership more as involving rather than imposing, because it reflects the commitment of a leader in the success of an operation and its execution. Not listening to team members is another pit of leadership, because it makes members feel neglected and frustrated in most cases. Other mistakes include avoiding responsibilities by over-tasking members, and not respecting them for who they are by not showing some element of trust in their relationship with them.

The bottom line remains, that there is no standard, sure formula, or method in being a successful manager or leader. Neither there is a standard mode of building and maintaining effective teams, because situations and environments differ from each other. However, the common attitudes which make a leader highly effective in leading others are: 1) Appreciating the collective intelligence of their team members; 2) Believing in the power of diversity among team members; 3) Seeing leadership as a call to serve with honesty and humility in the interest of all, and not as a position to be served, regardless of their office or power. Leaders should lead by coordinating, and not dominating others, and being realistic in all activities required to achieve a common purpose.

Being highly effective is all about taking control without being autocratic, applying the right principles at the right time in order to make things happen and go well. However, it's not enough to survive on one's strength, but always to strive for the best at all times.

While at a leadership conference in London, I came across a trademark for an organisation I dreamed of working for while I was a student many years ago. I joked with a university professor who also attended the conference about the same trademark, and then she opened up and talked about herself as a former employee of that same organisation. I asked her what went wrong, and she replied that when a leader thinks he knows and can do it all, he shamefully takes the trophy at the end of his one-horse race. She then went on and cleared the air by saying once certain vital aspects are not considered, there are bound to be problems. During lunch at the same conference, I decided to locate the professor who would know and understand the cause behind that event, which made a horse ride across seven seas before ending up drinking from a small river in the village unknown to it. My next question was what are the key aspects a leader must never joke about in order to remain highly effective. She replied, in most cases, business performance management enables leaders to see the organisation as a whole, instead of as a division, or sectional level, because it deals with the overall monitoring of vital functions, such as sales and marketing, human resources, supply chain management, accounting and finance—all of which have a huge role to play on the role of an organisation. In fact, Wayne Eckerson of The Data Warehouse Institute defines performance management as "a series of organisational processes and applications designed to optimize the execution of business strategy." Cost-based management is another aspect which an organisation can't survive without, because it's an approach for evaluating an organisation's activities over a certain period of time. In a nutshell, it serves as an indicator for an organisation's financial performance.

Cross-functional working is another aspect which is to be considered, because it helps organisations improve coordination and integration. It also creates a platform for spanning organisational boundaries, and reduces the production cycle time in new product development. Cross-functional working enables leaders to provide adequate support to overcome team formation issues, recognizing the talents and contributions of each individual's personal development.

Managing volatility is another core aspect which has always been challenging in many cases, because it requires the ability to handle crises and unexpected situations. Managers and leaders are advised to gain a better understanding of risk management. Alignment with the business strategy requires the ability of a leader to relate to people, operations, and strategy, for the purpose of perfect execution. Many thanks to the professor for the insight she shared with me. As I usually say, once upon a time is the beginning of every story; likewise, only if I had known that it is always the case at the end of every moment of ignorance. I only wished the professor had corrected the chief executive officer before playing the fool, but it's now an issue of medicine after death—too little too late.

CHAPTER 5

FACTORS FOR DRIVING HIGH-PERFORMANCE LEADERSHIP

In general, to remain highly effective, leaders need to know how best to use their leadership skills, such as decision making, delegation, motivation and effective communication to dramatically improve the performance of their team members. This includes being able to implement proven team building skills, knowing how best to coach, develop and support their team members for improved effectiveness, how to inspire a shared vision, set clear goals, objectives and performance standards, win commitment of members towards operational success, and how to create a realistic feedback process at regular intervals. Another point is seeking ways for improving financial performance by employing expertise to give accurate advice to keep an organisation floating financially.

The ability to make use of strategic thinking and planning techniques in gearing up for the future is a marginal advantage to every leader, because it creates a better platform for inspiring team members to achieve peak performance. The use of strategic thinking and planning provides leaders with insight for better direction on how to nurse an organisation's vision, values, and culture to uphold a better reputation within an industry. Another point about the importance of strategic thinking and planning is that it's helpful in developing a collaborative spirit while building effective teams. However, the major driving factors for a highly performing environment to take place, realistically and effectively, are

41

leadership, strategy and innovation, these three factors are the major tools an organisation requires to cut through the fog of new ideas and implement modern ways of getting things done.

Factor 1: Leadership

The major function of leadership in any organisation is the management and utilization of resources for an expected output. However, leadership as a whole depends on different skills, styles, attitudes and attributes in execution. In highly effective teams, another major of characteristic of leadership is readiness to adapt and encourage continuous change in which leaders need to challenge their members to ensure that they remain focused on delivering high performance while providing them with necessary support, such as coaching, training, feedback, advice, and recognition. Another fact is that leaders must know how best to develop and communicate a compelling vision across teams and the entire organisation. However, organisations intending to create a high-performance environment will probably already have a 360-degree leadership feedback process in place. Anyone leading an organisation without a vision is similar to three blind men being led by a blind man. Without precise direction, they would not all end in the same place if proper care is not taken. Another function of leadership for teams to remain highly effective is the regular evaluation of the team's objectives, output and effectiveness in ensuring that team members are on track to achieve their goals within an organisation time frame set for a project. Leaders have to hold team members accountable for their actions, having made clear their responsibility in line with reasonable expectations. Leadership facilitates the encouragement of new ideas and creativity, which are the best parameters for innovation. The encouragement of personal growth, influencing and negotiation skills are also functions of leadership in building and maintaining high-performance leadership within an organisation.

However, in recent years, the major challenge facing leadership in most organisations has been the inability of leaders to perform expert execution. This key challenge has a lot to do with their competency or technical skills to deliver exceptional service for their organisation. Temperament, which combines the maturity and judgment of a leader, facilitates the ability to establish clear direction for the organisation, and maintains a strong relationship with stakeholders. In a nutshell, being oneself and seeking ways to improve one's skills is the best way to lead and carry others along.

Factor 2: Strategy

The major function of having a strategy within any team or organisation is to build a platform for achieving its vision, and to clearly define a pathway for getting there. In reality, for any leader to be successful, he or she would have to focus more on the use of strategic thinking and execution parameters, which include planning the best for the future in terms of utilizing available resources to remain leaders within the industry. However, the position of strategy includes setting a vision, a process and systems which would support the strategy in getting things done by making realistic decisions. Without the alignment of people and operations for an organisational strategy, the whole situation becomes meaningless. In making a strategy meaningful, leaders should ensure it is made up of reasonable values, principles, approaches, techniques and models, which could help it stand the test of time. In addition, it needs the ability to adjust and change when necessary in order to be effective, productive and highly profitable.

In formulating a reasonable strategy, leaders should always consider the impact of knowledge, technology, and competitive analytical tools from different sources to help both leaders and the organisation in edging out rivals and maintaining a better position within any industry. The demand for innovative products and services is increasing more ever than before. Leaders are always in need of updated ideals in designing and formulating strategies to meet current challenges. Whether now or later, it's a good for the leader to survive and thrive to attain and maintain a good position within any given industry, especially in a fast-changing world, yet leaders and organisations must work more on strategy by teaming up. They must think outside the box in order to out-perform their competitors before being outpaced by their competitors. As an executive coach, I strongly believe in the beauty of teamwork, because without it, both leaders and their strategies would end up meaningless. As a matter of fact, leaders need to build authentic relationships which need to be based on trust, honesty, and transparency to make strategy meaningful.

Factor 3: Innovation

Innovation in high-performance leadership deals with ambiguity and continuous change within an organisation. It creates the capacity to challenge the traditional system in executing strategic plans. As a matter of fact, innovation is commitment to the continuous review and improvement of an organisation's operational system.

For innovation to be visible, realistic and achievable within an organisation, the role of a change agent cannot be underestimated. Change agents serve as the major brain for creative thinking, with a major focus on developing the major capability to adapt and encourage continuous change.

Building and maintaining high-performance teams is the core responsibility of effective leadership, which needs to embrace and innovate in the face of changing environments and contexts. However, seeking innovative ideals is the best way to move an organisation forward and to foil competitors within an industry. However, the presence of an effective leader needs to produce a reasonable amount of impact and outcome for an organisation that is eventually linked in sharing innovative values and culture for both the short- and long-term objectives.

Embracing innovation is a better way of helping an organisation handle huge operational costs due to modern ways of handling and utilizing available resources. However, on the other hand, it also helps in creating and building the required capabilities and competencies needed to gain appropriate and sustained competitive advantages. Innovation creates a better platform for an organisation to be more successful via learning at both at individual and group stages, which is a perfect avenue to spread initiatives.

For leaders to create an environment which fosters high performance, it needs to encourage the flow of new ideas to solve complex problems, which is an essential tool for effectively driving and managing change by creating a plan which is capable of eradicating barriers to high performance within an organisation. Innovation can never be achieved without a leader applying the principles of effective communication, which should be seen as the ability to disseminate information for stakeholders, and understanding and diffusing negative emotions. However, leaders need to make use of communication to encourage high performance by improving their ability to influence and collaborate with stakeholders via effective negotiation skills, which are necessary to draw and maintain a reasonable balance for both internal and external stakeholders' interests. It's also required to drive a reasonable strategic direction in the interest of all stakeholders.

Effective leadership begins with extensive knowledge of what needs to be done when knowing the strengths and weaknesses of team members, and represents the major platform for high performance. Effective leaders always give serious consideration to resource allocation, scheduling, professional development, funding, and procurement.

CHAPTER 6

ENCOURAGING A HIGH-PERFORMANCE ENVIRONMENT

Having a nice car is one thing; maintaining it in a reasonable manner is another. It's one thing for leaders to make team members understand and acknowledge what is expected of them, which is a platform for motivation and getting things done at any given time, but it's another thing for the same leader to create a conducive environment by making sure team members are being supported towards achieving organisational goals. However, it is up to leaders to ensure that team members are being treated fairly in terms of recognising and valuing their contributions towards the success of the organisation as a whole.

Leaders need to respect the emotions and ideas of their members due their skills and experience, because without those, the position of a leader or manager is of little use within an organisation. As a matter of fact, being a leader or manager does not mean things will be done without team members.

I was once told by Mr Franck Ledbetter, a former fire service manager, and now a training consultant, that managers should be delighted to see their front line officers developing themselves as a result of career progression and personal development. Such managers only need to motivate by assigning front line officers some roles to help improve their skills and confidence. It also makes it easier for organisations to develop and prepare potential managers to carry on organisational operations without the cost of recruiting and training new managers. In other words, giving the required and necessary support to team members is a better way of encouraging a high-performance team due to the in-depth level of understanding and handling of operations they will acquire.

In encouraging a high-performance environment, leaders can never underestimate the importance of planning, due to its impact in strategizing the process of operations. Planning creates a platform to map out the critical process of identifying and selecting an improvement process for various operations within an organisation. Ahead of organizing and implementing strategies and parameters for improvements, planning remains the key and principal issue, because it tells what to be done, along with where, when, and how things needed to be done, which plays a critical role in designing the vision and mission of any organisation. However, encouraging a high-performance environment requires the preparation of a performance analysis of an organisation, so as to indicate where improvement is to be carried out. One major fact that I realize as an executive coach is that it's the major responsibility of a leader to ensure that the team has adequate skills, knowledge, and other reasonable parameters, such as information and required resources, to accomplish tasks assigned to them. Remaining stagnant is the worst of all situations a leader and his team members can experience in terms of implementing of the same strategic plan without change, and getting the same result, which may be insufficient or incapable of defeating competition and maintaining a better place within the industry. As a matter of fact, leaders need to evaluate their plans on a continuous basis, which is the cornerstone for improvement.

Organizing is another parameter to be considered when encouraging any high-performance environment, because it is comprised of organisational design, culture and networks, which are internal core parameters for effective performance. In a nutshell, organisational design ensures that an organisation's inner system fits its primary purpose, and ensures that it's capable and supportive for leadership transformation, which is required to enhance cultural vitality and operational excellence. Good organisation design promotes integrity, wholeness, and operational dexterity by answering critical questions regarding an organisation's value. Organizing affects the designing of an organisation's products and services in terms of the value attached to them, in terms of what is produced or rendered, which class of customers the product fits, and the purpose of production which supports the creation of the unique value of the product.

The approach and manner of fulfilling the unique needs of customers are distinctive aspects in organizing, because they allow stakeholders to choose what they think is best in creating uniqueness and value for the customer's money. However, the choices must be seen as reliable for an organisation to uphold its reputation for the best public recognition, which is a better platform to attract more investors to boost the organisation's financial position. Leaders need to ensure that the components of their organisation are made up of the alignment of structure and strategy, people and processes, leadership and culture, measurement and control, which are vital parameters in attaining success.

Components of an Organisation:

Structure: This refers to how members within an organisation are organised in relation to its operations, and how they relate to each other, which could be hierarchical, horizontal or in matrix format.

Strategy: According to Johnson and Scholes in their book, *Exploring Corporate Strategy,* strategy is the direction and scope of an organisation over the long-term. It achieves an advantage for the organisation through its configuration of resources within a challenging environment, in order to meet the needs of markets and to fulfil stakeholder expectations.

People: This is the major organisational factor, which plays a very important role in the fulfilment of organisational goals, with available resources, and by sharing the required task in making strategy a reality.

Processes: This is the collections ideas, tasks and activities that come together for the purpose of transforming input into output within an organisation.

Leadership: This generally involves the organizing and direction of people to perform various tasks. It owes stakeholders a huge form of accountability for the allocation and utilization of resources and other factors in relation to the expected aims and objectives.

Culture: This is the major philosophy that reflects the various approaches in which an organisation conducts its business. This includes the way it treats its employees, customers, and the wider community, as well as the extent to which freedom is allowed in decision- making, developing new ideas, and personal expression. Culture also determines how power and information flow through its hierarchy, and how committed employees are towards collective objectives.

Control: This is the vital parameter within an organisation which all organisational and operational processes are in proper alignment toward achieving the desired outcome. It ensures that organisational and operational plans are carried out the way they were designed. Its major purpose is to ensure customer satisfaction in its outputs. However, the above components are no joking matters for any serious minded leader, because the above components would reflect more of the capability, competence, skills and knowledge towards achieving and encouraging high-performance leadership.

A friend of mine once told me that he considers it shameful stetting down for half braked bread, because there is danger in consuming it and it can't be exchanged for another item. In other words, it's better for leaders to be dedicated to excellence by aiming for the best in whatever they are expecting in relationship to their performance. However, being dedicated to greater achievements as a leader is a better way of impacting and inspiring team members to build, encourage and maintain a high-performance environment. Leading team members with inspiration is an act of carrying them along without force or sanctions; this gives leadership real meaning based on the ability to influence members, mostly in complex situations.

INFLUENCE AND COLLABORATION: NEGOTIATION

For leaders to be seen as being capable by others, they would have been consistent and reliable in all their relationships and activities with others within an organisation. This capability seen by others would be a result of the leader's commitment toward achieving organisational goals. The theme influence and collaboration reflects the huge role leaders play in the smooth running of an organisation, which requires them to be more approachable in influencing and negotiating with both internal and external stakeholders for mutual and strategic benefits. In a nutshell, influence and collaboration are both platforms that deal with essential organisational parameters, such as power, politics, persuasion, and strategy implementation for goal achievement. It is wise for leaders to identify their potential challenges before knowing how best to influence stakeholders with respect to their strategic implementation plans for execution.

Leaders need to study situations before making an attempt to influence their members, because it enables them to feel they are being treated professionally, and with respect. Leaders need to clearly establish that they believe in the strength and the ability of their team members, which is another way of building trust and confidence within a team. This also helps them with the ability to tap into potential for higher levels in their careers. Recognizing and rewarding the efforts of team members is another way to gain the most of their ability in getting things done in an exceptional manner. Having the required skills to influence others is better than the use of power on a continuous basis, because it makes team members see leaders as being political and aggressive, which affects the smooth running of an operation in the long run. This happens because team members see themselves as being used, and later lose interest in the job. As a matter of fact, commitment could then be missing in the team dynamics, and achieving peak performance could become a serious struggle. However, the ability to influence creates room for leaders to identify and understand the major concerns of team members as a result of effective communication. Moreover, it creates a better presence to communicate major concerns clearly and powerfully, while communicating credibly and factually with all staff for maximum understanding.

It becomes easier to make reasonable and effective decisions because it would be in perfect line with members' concerns. Leaders need to gain awareness of their influencing style, i.e., skills and capabilities which would enable them build a deeper appreciation and understanding of the role of influence in both team and organisational management. The importance of acquiring effective influencing skills would enable leaders to negotiate their way toward better relationships via learning new techniques and exercises, which would also be useful in resolving conflicts within an organisation.

COLLABORATION

The importance of collaboration is for team members to pull and share ideas in cooperation to accomplish organisational goals within a specific time frame. In other words, it's a platform for leaders to connect their team members via internal social networks in a transparent manner. Collaboration is a platform for members to support and correct each other's mistakes; however, the level of collaboration within a team reflects how responsible a leader is. Collaboration as a whole enables leaders to sharpen their organisation's communication capabilities, creating greater access to their intellectual assets, i.e., team members, which increase the flexibility and responsiveness of an organisation. Collaboration also enables an organisation to be more productive and effective in the areas of knowledge sharing and transfer, identifying and creating new opportunities, businesses growth and appreciation for different cultures, mostly in a multinational organisation.

Collaboration and teamwork create an avenue for collective knowledge, resources and skills for an organisation to flourish in meeting stakeholders' expectations, which typically facilitate large-scale production and open positive negotiation outcomes by creating win-win situations. Effective collaboration within an organisation enables leaders to achieve higher quality outcomes in terms of service delivery However, focusing on the value of collaboration can motivate team members in developing themselves for better opportunities.

During a Christian leaders' summit held in London some years ago, Bishop Moses Martins said, "You can't just do it alone; you need your team members' helping hands in executing your beautiful strategy by building networks and coalitions." It's reasonable to understand the principles behind networking and identify opportunities that would be in everyone's interests in making collaboration and strategy implementation more effective, which is part of improving oneself.

Both influence and collaboration enable leaders to inspire, persuade, and win over the resistors in a changing environment. Persuasion requires leaders to communicate with, an impact members to see the big picture clearly, and buy a leader's idea to get their commitment on board. It's paramount for leaders to be assertive in identifying the potential issues and conditions for resistance, the different types of resistors, and how to best handle them along with learning more effective persuasion techniques which requires that one be an effective negotiator.

EFFECTIVE NEGOTIATION

Picture yourself on a mission to get two diamond rings from the mouth of a lion in the town unknown to you. Getting those diamond rings would fetch you 100 million pounds, a knight grand cross, which is the highest grade in many orders of knighthood, and an influential personality. The mission terms and conditions require that the lion must remain alive after you've gotten those diamond rings from its mouth, and there is a possibility that the lion might have swallowed one of the rings. Saying no is also an option. The question is: what would you do?

A friend of mine told me it's a huge challenge, and one needs to be seriously prepared. So, likewise, negotiation is not a platform for playing in the gallery, i.e., seeking cheap popularity and recognition. It's a platform to make all applicable tactics and strategies in achieving and attaining reasonable concessions regarding committable agreement.

Negotiation as matter of fact remains inevitable in running both teams and organisations. It remains the platform for "give and take," i.e., mutual benefits. However, everyday negotiation situations are becoming more complex in deal making in an attempt to get better results in every situation. Negotiation as a whole is a practice-oriented field; leaders can't do without having the skills and techniques to engage in bargain making with team members and other stakeholders. For leaders to be effective negotiators, there is a big need to understand the process of negotiation in the first place. After that, the goal is to maintain a better focus on the challenges experienced at different stages of the negotiation process, which requires a well-equipped leader to apply different skills and techniques for each stage, depending on the expectations and potential outcomes of each stage. The leader's ability to gather relevant facts, figures, and documents needed to back up negotiation points would help in gaining greater edge and a better position in the deal.

The ability to set a reasonable time frame to reach an agreement regarding specific terms attached to a negotiation process is a critical factor. Leaders need to create a plan for the possibility of both sides having a fair deal in the negotiation process. However, every negotiator needs to be sensitive and realistic at the negotiation table, mostly when counterparts seem to be stronger, and have more leverage regarding a situation, because when you swim with sharks, never smell blood, or else the story changes. In any struggle, as negotiator, you should learn how best to keep your head safe, because if broken, it remains yours.

Having read a lot of books and publications on negotiation, and relating it to my personal experience as a business coach, negotiation is a process which includes the following strategies:

SETTING CLEAR GOALS:

For a negotiation to succeed, leaders need have a clear sense of what they really want as an expected outcome. Goal setting is a parameter for measuring success or failure in any negotiation process. Having a goal in mind enables leaders to make the best preparations ahead of time; in other words, to bargain the best deals for their organisations. It's advisable for leaders to enter into negotiations with specific goals, and also with a clear understanding of what might be of interest and mutual benefit to both parties. Think ahead about what might be the next and best alternative in case talks break down. However, it's better for leaders to think of potential situations that could place them in a better and stronger position in any deal. Being reasonable and having a critical thinking of likely possible outcome is advisable when setting goals, otherwise one would end up being caught up in the middle, which would force one to give more in exchange for less.

Goal setting is a way of avoiding dispute and confusion. Know what each party intends to achieve based on their relevance and importance in making strategic choices. Goal setting makes it easier to examine the fundamental questions regarding the negotiation process, which serves as a reasonable parameter in achieving success. Some of these are:

1)   What does each party need from the deal?
2)   What is each party's position in the deal?

Regardless of the situation, leaders should always ensure that their goal setting is SMART, Specific, Measurable, Attainable, Relevant, and Time-bound. The more leaders can clarify their goals in a negotiation process, the more they are likely to attain them.

RESEARCHING INTERESTS AND ALTERNATIVES FOR PARTIES

This is a better way of negotiating for better outcomes while at the same time protecting relationships and reputations for other strategic benefits. Note: not holding the better and stronger position in an existing deal does not make one a failure; rather, it prepares for better opportunities and greater challenges in the field of negotiation. In most cases, creating a checklist of issues that need to be addressed according to a scale of preference would help facilitate an understanding of each other's positions regarding various situations at the negotiation table, and could expedite the negotiation.

However, researching the interests and alternatives of both parties requires leaders to first identify their strengths and work on their weaknesses with the aim of reducing the opportunities of their counterpart. This increases their threats in order to accomplish a better position in any deal, including having a lot of information about the deal and their counterpart's weaknesses.

It's better for leaders to be creative when seeking other options in which would enable them to increase their bargaining power in any deal. Effective negation is never a one- man game, because it requires a collection of ideals, skills, experience, professionalism and brainstorming with other key players within an organisation.

I remember a world leader once addressing senior executives in the aviation sector on minimizing plane crashes, telling them to think outside the box while dealing with the situation. In other words, it's better for leaders to endeavour to expand their research to increase their options regarding a deal. However, failing to have available options during a negotiation is simply unwise. Having a good alternative empowers leaders with the confidence to either reach a mutually satisfactory agreement, or walk away to a better alternative.

EXPLORING A STRATEGY

This is a major aspect of any negotiation process that requires the act of a forward thinking of a leader to enhance effective preparation by considering all possible outcomes. This pre-determined approach or prepared plan of action to achieve a specific goal or objective to potentially find and make an agreement in a negotiation with another party. However, planning is the most important activity in any negotiation exercise, but while planning, leaders should be realistic in knowing their limits and available alternatives. Planning one's strategy for negotiation requires the ability of a leader to facilitate negotiation success by organizing, briefing, and leading his negotiation team in preparation for negotiation or win-win outcomes. In the real sense of effective preparation, it's the major responsibility of leaders to ensure that they've gotten all information and details required to avoid incompetence at the negotiation table. They have to possess the ability to gather, organize, and retain relevant, accurate information related to the negotiation process. They also need the ability to read and understand technical and audit reports, and other related records, which serve as indicators. Leaders must be able to communicate orally, and in writing. The ability to think creatively and recognize new and unique approaches for effective negotiations is a mandatory requirement. They also need the ability to maintain honesty and integrity in all activities related to the process. While planning ahead for any negotiation process, it is necessary to set targets, and also knowing where to start, so as to avoid playing the hard ball game during the negotiation process. Never should leaders deflect from their original plans lest more would be exchanged for less.

EXCHANGING INFORMATION

This is known as the exploration stage in negotiation, because it remains the point where information is being shared with others within the organisation, with the aim of learning more about their counterparts, and what they want in the deal. The major purpose of exchanging information is to iron out the major issues of concern which includes making reference to the past of an organisation relating to the present leading to the future. However, this stage needs to be carefully and properly planned, because it deals with a high level of sensitivity, where leaders need to know what to say, and when to and how to conduct themselves when exchanging information to avoid manipulation. In most cases, experience learned at this stage can always be applied in other situations within an organisation.

Exchanging information is not just a matter of discovering information, but rather a climate for the subsequent negotiation to make future situations easier. In a nutshell, the exchanging of information gives leaders an insight into exploring the needs, interests, and underlying assumptions of both sides. My stand never changes at point, *something for something, nothing for nothing.*

OPENING THE NEGOTIATION

Negotiators start by identifying issues of common concern, and perhaps agreement. This enables them to build confidence in tackling difficult situations. In most cases it's always a game of hide and seeks, by allowing the other party speak first to identify their strengths and strategy in order to know what to reveal at any particular point in time. There are situations whereby one would need to speak first, which gives the opportunity to "anchor" the negotiations by providing information or positions that others respond to. However, the opening stage involves the leader's ability to communicate their interested clearly and openly. They also need to be willing to know more about their counterpart's counter-presentations. This stage in negotiation involves having a clear strategy, working out contingencies and deciding most of the parameters of the subsequent discussions.

However, leaders need to ensure that issues on the negotiation table are tenderable, reasonable and negotiable. For a negotiation session to be successful, both parties must believe that there are acceptable settlement options that are possible as a result of participation in the process. The opening stage in any negotiation process is very vital, because it's a point where building trustworthy relationships with the other party becomes the principal key. Without trust, the hard ball game remains. As a matter of fact, one would have to pay through his nose to attain a better and more reasonable position in any negotiation process. Trust enables parties to reach an agreement faster, and with less resistance and time-consuming inquisition. Building trust involves the full disclosure all of the facts surrounding the negotiation process, and other parameters that are likely to occur regarding the situation.

BARGAINING TO CREATE REASONABLE VALUE

This is the major point where concessions are given on reasonable terms and conditions; however, this is also the heart of any negotiation process. Leaders need to value both what is being given and received regarding the situation in terms of its strategic importance. Conflict often arises at this point in the negotiation process, due to the use of tactics, and the pressure of meeting stakeholders' expectations. Leaders need to be diplomatic in making arrangements and agreements before committing to a contractual obligation.

As a matter of fact it's paramount that leaders draft a win – win strategy that will enable a reasonable deal for both sides, rather than one party compromising, which can cause a breakdown in the negotiation process.

CLOSING DEALS WITH COMMITMENT

Leaders should always avoid cheating the other side out of a fair deal, or attempting to trick the other side into agreeing by giving them false information, inadequate or misleading facts and figures, or by using scare tactics. This act creates an atmosphere of mistrust, and is counter-productive to reaching a resolution. It can lead to contracts being terminated with the possibility of seeking compensation. Trying to bring a negotiation process to an end on a fast track with the assumption that things are settled, i.e., acting on the grounds of pretence is a dangerous move, as issues might later backfire. In a nutshell, both parties need to be sure what they agreed on at the closing point, by ensuring that all parties have a better deal.

As a matter of fact and reality, closing is a process of gaining validation and acceptance, rather than forcing agreement. Each party may require different means to accomplish their part in reaching a fair deal, in which the critical factor remains that the approach must be built on respect, understanding, and mutuality among stakeholders and other parties to the negotiation process.

A client of mine told me of his former company's loss of a huge contract, along with their reputation due to their breach of trust with local authorities. They were invited to make a tender for the enforcement of their parking services when the service was experiencing a high level of mismanagement, and the only alternative was to contract it out for better control and accountability. Having informed all stakeholders, including the trade union, it was agreed that the enforcement officers would remain on their existing contract. But, having followed due process, the service was contracted out, and the company began to experience a problem in paying staff their entitlements, and meeting their contractual obligations. The company began to seek various ways to change or terminate the contracts of existing staff, with the aim of hiring cheap labour, but the trade union made up its strength in protecting the interest of its members. This included other staff members that were forced by the situation to join the union due to the "no mercy" policy being implemented. As a matter of fact, the contractors claimed to be transparent in welcoming anyone to their terms and conditions.

At the end of three months, none of the staff were interested, so it became a game of force due to the poor financial state of the business, but the local authorities, who sat on the fence, believed the process was open and that staff could make a choice. While staff were about to be called in and forced to sign up for low terms and conditions, the trade union was informed about the situation, but there was no hard proof.

The trade union decided to let a young, sharp member of staff pretend to be ready to sign up the new terms, and pass a copy of the contract terms and conditions through the window. The moment the council leader saw the document, he terminated the contract immediately to avoid public anger. As a matter of fact, the local council took back their staff, and there was a need to streamline jobs within the contract's company to reduce overhead costs after losing a huge business alongside another in a neighbouring council due to the news of mistrust and damage of reputation.

Furthermore, without the required and updated negotiation skills, there is no way a leader can be a good negotiator. Negotiation skills are the required and the applicable strategies and techniques necessary to negotiate effective deals within parties. Negotiation skills are taught at most business schools, and some specialized/professional training centres. However, effective negotiation requires a variety of skills drawn from different disciplines which includes: communication, persuasion and influence, planning, strategizing, tactics, process and systems networks, teamwork, and others.

As a matter of fact, negotiation requires much face-to-face interaction, and not by phone, internet or via fax. Leaders need to understand in real context effective negotiation skills cannot be learned by just reading, but requires active participation, and learning directly from experts in the field of negotiation.

A major challenge in negotiation as a whole represents the ability of leaders to manage their relationships with other parties, managing their emotions and impulses, and steadily working toward the goal. In a nutshell, negotiation has to be in line with set goals, which requires the right negotiation strategy in the context of parties being dealt with. Effective negotiation skills involve leaders choosing the best and most relevant negotiation style appropriate for the situation on board. Leaders need to be mature in their conflict handling style, because it goes miles in determining the level of interactivity and the creativity of a bargaining style. It serves as a platform for identifying opportunities for win-win situations in all negotiation processes.

Having a good strategy for negotiation is one thing, and having the skills and competencies to execute those strategies as a good negotiator is another. However, the characteristics of a good negotiator include the ability to remain charming under pressure, and apply effective listening skills, patience; being specific, assertive, persuasive, and perseverant. Negotiators also need the ability to express thoughts verbally, to be flexible, approachable, with the ability to think fast about a situation, and also have insight into possible outcomes for any decision concluded in any negotiation process.

The general fact about encouraging a high-performance environment depends on the leader's ability to empower and develop a vision for his teams. According to business dictionary.com, empowerment is referred to as the management practice of sharing information, rewards, and power among team members, with the purpose and ability of taking initiative and making decisions to solve problems and improving their skills. In this scenario, the operation and the overall performance always remain the paramount objective of any organisation. Empowerment is a platform for making team members more responsible by assigning those roles which help them build their competence and confidence.

Empowerment enables leaders to maintain a good relationship by creating various ways of improving team members in areas such as: knowledge and skills, resources and utilizing opportunities, motivation, and being accountable for the outcomes of their actions.

Empowerment gives team member the legitimate authority to act on behalf of the organisation, regardless of the position or role within an organisation. However, leaders need to understand that empowerment should be in line with the needs of both internal and external stakeholders, mostly in terms of meeting customer's needs. Therefore, relevant and accurate information needs to be supplied at the appropriate time and to the appropriate personnel to facilitate the proper decision-making.

Having discussed empowerment, I would like to discuss developing a vision. Leaders should understand clearly that a vision represents the future they wish to create, mostly for themselves and their organisations. However, when leaders' aspirations are set out clearly and with confidence, they become a powerful tool for communicating what they want to achieve for their organisation within a reasonable and specific time, with all hands on deck.

For a vision to be made realistic, it's paramount for leaders to understand themselves, their vision, and the purpose for the vision. However, the purpose of every vision is always relieved by the issues it helps mankind solve, and not the conflict it creates. Leaders should always seek strategies in making their vision a reality and also improving outcomes on a continuous basis, which is the best way to value the competence within a workforce, and build confidence in it.

A vision needs to be realistic in order to formulate the right strategy in developing the right workforce, which is a critical factor in getting things done. In simple terms, leaders need to have a clear vision, be realistic about challenges, and inspire and support team members in delivering the desired outcomes for the organisation as a whole. A vision needs to be shared with other stakeholders within an organisation, or else the situation can place a leader in a one-horse race, which is of no value to stakeholders.

The main purpose of having and sharing a vision with team members and other stakeholders is to reflect transparency and a leader's values and respect for them by giving a sense of belonging by allowing them to take part in decision-making processes, which enables them to support such leaders in achieving expected goals.

However, sharing a vision makes it more sensible, and reflects the leader's openness, honesty, and responsibility in terms of the quality of the potential achievement.

CHAPTER 7

DISCOVERING ONE'S STRENGTHS

"Where there is no struggle, there is no strength." ~Oprah Winfrey
I remember during my school days, how I had to work extra hours to pay my fee, my house rent, council tax, and other utilities. I needed to attend class at the expense of certain bonuses, while other colleagues made their full package at the end of every quarter. I had to work twelve hours most Sundays for the same rate just to meet up my contracted hours, while others would work the same Sunday for a *double pay*. I also remember the manager once told me, *"I know you are giving up today's pleasure for tomorrow's comfortability.* The struggle was that I gave up a lot of friends, parties, and other outings in search of my goal and direction. However, the investment towards one's goal in attaining a specific and realistic direction, mostly in light of limited resources such as money and time, always requires a serious struggle to attain.

I'm deeply inspired by Oprah Winfrey's quote because the outcome of every struggle always justifies the strength of a leader in terms of his ability and capability. However, both indicate how successful a leader is, and would be, mostly in terms of handling risk, crisis, challenges, and utilizing resources in attaining goals.

I believe there is great ability in a leader's strengths and talents in terms of what he can achieve in both the short and long run. He can also go places in his career, mostly when he remains focused, and capitalizes on them. A better approach to identify one's strength is a recommended model, known as the DISC approach. Taking an in-depth look into the approach would provide a platform to understand more effectively some paramount parameters in discovering more about a leader's strength, which enables the establishment of leadership as a whole. The approach explains four main components of leadership: Dominance, Influence, Steadiness and Compliance, in describing a leader's strengths and weaknesses.

Understanding the DISC approach makes one a better leader, a better communicator, and more able to engage others in decision-making processes, which helps gain more strength from developing others and making them more effective. The DISC approach reflects more in terms of the law of growth, which enhances the challenge of leaders to improve themselves as they move on in their respective careers.

DOMINANCE

In general, dominance is defined as a relationship between individuals that is established through a believed priority and accepted chain of command in terms of access regarding specific desires, situations and resources within an organisation. Leaders who believe in dominance tend have their strengths in achieving results regardless of what it takes, and are change-oriented by giving all it takes to meet expectations or targets. They are good at directing all operational processes by avoiding wastage in terms of available resources, and are self-determined toward delivering excellent performance, regardless of the outcome.

Leaders with dominant behaviours are often characterized by having a clear line of legitimate authority to operate, control and delegate functions to others. Such leaders believe so much in the power conferred on them, but the weakness aspect of being dominant makes a leader more demanding. In many cases, they may not be concerned with the outcome of their team members, and this act can make team members feel less motivated in carrying on with such leaders, because their future seems to be uncertain. The demanding attitude of such leaders can make team members lose their zeal in giving their best performance to meet organisational objectives. Another weak aspect of dominance in a leader is insensitivity, which makes others believe them to be heartless, inconsiderate, and without concern for others from the way they plan, delegate and execute strategies. However, such leaders are well known for creating win/lose situations in most negotiation situations.

INFLUENCE

Successful leaders never think of themselves alone, but rather, think of making others successful along with themselves. A well-experienced sport coach can't do it all without his team's joint effort, as a matter of fact he needs to build a better relationship to influence and persuade his players to put in their best while on the pitch. John Maxwell describes the Law of Influence as the true test of a leader in creating a positive change within an organisation. In a nutshell, he describes leadership as the act of influencing people, nothing more or less. Influence is a serious parameter in leading others, because it requires leaders to always be ready to give something bigger than themselves off themselves in the interest of all. However, these include *character* in terms of their personality, *relationships* with stakeholders within an origination, *knowledge* in terms what they know, i.e., skills, experience, education and training regarding a specific profession or situation within an organisation. It also includes their *ability* in terms of what they can do in tough times and in unexpected situations, which ends up reflecting a leader's strength.

The ability of a leader to influence others requires a high level of maturity and integrity for others to trust him and see him as a respectable figure. However, optimism makes a leader smarter when handling diplomatic and strategic issues, with the aim of achieving the best possible outcome in any situation in the interest of an organisation. Furthermore, optimistic leaders raise the aspirations of others to achieve their individual potentials via speaking possibilities in terms of what they can attain and achieve in their respective fields, by focusing on more innovative approaches in solving problems through creative thinking.

Influential leaders are always visionary in all their undertakings, by having a deeper insight into strategic issues affecting an organisation. Visionary leaders are open to the latest information in terms of recent facts and figures, which are useful parameters in making relevant and reasonable decisions, which also keeps them updated about external factors which affect the operational activities of their organisations. It's reasonable for leaders to constantly search for additional information, lest they become locked from the rest of the world. Visionary leaders are highly sensitive, and have the ability to see things with their mind's eye, often long before others, which enables them to study situations and make good predictions in a relevant manner.

Visionary leadership empowers team members to be strong while facing challenges despite the odds, because they know what they are doing, and what they want to achieve. The facts remain that a vision lives longer than the one who discovered it. When the word "visionary" is mentioned, people probably think of great leaders, i.e., someone who inspires through ground-breaking ideas expertly communicated, but visionary leadership is a matter of making progressive steps one at a time, which makes a leader's journey more meaningful. Vision as a powerful element in a leader's mind-set creates the vitality in them which makes them strong and courageous while facing turbulent times and challenges. This makes them focus on the required energy such as skills and knowledge to execute strategies and attain the expected direction. A clear vision makes it easier to explain to stakeholders the main purpose of their vision in the reality of solving organisational issues.

The mission of influencing others remains impossible without a leader being an excellent communicator, because it remains the most important key to leadership success. Good communication makes it convenient for leaders in clarifying the purpose of their vision, and enables stakeholders to get their message. Effective communication enables leaders to demonstrate their strong commitment and confidence, mostly in times of change, in attaining effectiveness in the outcomes. The ability to influence makes a leader more passionate in all they do, because it allows them to achieve more than they expect, mostly with the love and support they get from others. It enables them to break the bar of limitations in attaining greater heights. The downside of influence in most leaders is the act of ignoring warning signs by not considering previous experience in terms of people misinterpreting their vision and statement for something else. Sometimes, they have to learn from previous experience what would help them mount the right platform while dealing with people within their organisation to avoid being misunderstood and having their personality taken for granted. Another weakness in influencing people is that they are seen to talk actively, because influencing others requires the ability to communicate a lot in some cases to make their audience understand, and to gain their support to achieve the required change level to move their origination forward.

A friend of mine shared his experience with me with when first appointed as a non-executive director in a multinational gas company. He believed the strategic implementation model of the company was somehow outdated, involving a lot inconvenience, so he decided to recommend a change in the strategic implementation model to the chief executive officer, who later brought him on board to explain it to the directors. Having answered a lot of questions, he was seen as impulsive due to his passionate stance about his intended strategy, which was the result of his belief that they were incompetent. After suffering a huge meltdown in sales, the company decided to launch his strategy in the long run. To cut long story short, it took my friend a huge challenge before being able influence the board regarding his implementation ideas.

STEADINESS

This is the ability of a leader to remain firm in terms of using his strength in attaining a perfect direction. This ability requires a leader to be more reliable in all his undertakings, which makes others take him seriously. The positive aspect of leaders being steadfast makes them more consistent, great listeners, and dependable and loyal to all organisational stakeholders at any point in time, regardless of any situation that might occur.

Steadiness in a leader makes one thoughtful and accepting others the way they are. Even when tempered, they still accommodate others, believing the situation will improve. Steadiness goes along with patience in a leader when responding to situations. The fact remains that leaders need to be steadfast in order to execute both the strategies and visions of an organisation. Leaders also need to inspire stakeholders to work together in order to move things forward as smoothly as possible, which reflects the beauty of a leader's strength.

As often said, there is a limit to the human ability as to maintain checks and balances. In most cases, steadfast leaders are seen as being overly tolerant when team members are resistant to change when their understanding and support is needed to move the organisation forward. Steadfast leaders often believe in slow and steady wins the race, which others may see as out of sync with modern day technology in getting things done. Maturity is a psychological platform that aids steadfastness in leaders, because it gives them ability to respond to stakeholders in an appropriate manner.

COMPLIANCE

This is a major platform in ensuring that implementation and execution are in accordance with appropriate standards, and in line with relevant legislation, to ensure that activities are absolutely correct and acceptable. Compliance is a form of guideline for accountability in any professional field, such as accountancy, law, engineering, and architecture, because it sets the guidelines for professional ethics.

In an organisational context, the major purpose of compliance is to lay the perfect and accurate framework for driving perfect performance via standard ethics to guide executives in building plans that help minimize exposure to risk, and save time and money for a better result in the long run. Compliance as a whole requires competent personnel to drive stakeholders in a legal and standard manner. The major challenge in compliance is the updated and essential knowledge and skills necessary to identify and assess the impact of potential risks that might face an organisation. Leaders need to draft a detailed and task oriented policy to enhance perfect compliance.

The major function of compliance in leadership within an organisation is to ensure the safety, consistency, and high quality in the operations and delivery of excellence in an organisation's products and services. This ensures the company's ability to build and maintain a better reputation, which enables it to secure a better position in the competitive market.

In discovering one's strength for any leadership positions, it's paramount for leaders to understand the impact of strategic planning, which requires them to have foresight regarding their activities. However, strategic planning enables the ability to translate visions into realistic business strategies and processes for the purpose of perfect execution. Another aspect leader's face is managing their co-workers, mostly the difficult ones who never want to compromise their stand where necessary in the interest of others. However, the required strength in such situations includes the ability to remain calm while under pressure, treat others in a fair and impartial manner, and also communicate effectively to ensure a high level of productivity.

One good thing about leaders discovering their strengths at the right time is that it enhances effective team dynamics, because a creative ideal from one member might be analysed better by another with better analytical skills which could later morph into an effective strategy that could be implemented in attaining a leadership position in any completive environment. The 2014 FIFA World Cup was the 20th FIFA World Cup, which was hosted by Brazil and won by the German term, whose head coach, Joachim Löw, had been part of the team for over ten years,. I believe beyond a reasonable doubt that he would understand the ins and outs of the team better than anyone else, because he knows the ability and capability of each player, and how to use their strengths to coordinate and utilise each of them in right place at the right time for an excellent result based on his years of experience over the years as both assistant and head coach. In attaining an expected result, it's up to any leader to work on their weakness as much as they can to reduce damages affecting their strengths later, producing a less befitting outcome or result, similar to a football match where the midfielders and strikers are more focused on scoring as many goals as possible to win a qualifying series while the central defender is passing backwards at the time the midfielders are expecting a reasonable pass to make some strategic moves toward winning the game. The central defender's contribution would affect the team dynamics by frustrating the intention and ability of other team members. It's then up to the head coach to take a leader's position to sense the performance of the central defenders and the potential risk to the team performance on both short and long run, either to correct the central defender or substitute for another, because the outcome of his struggle is paramount to him and the players as a whole. The head coach needs to understand that the more he uses his strength in the midst of any struggle, i.e., the application of experience, skills and strategy in winning matches and tournaments, the more heights he mounted in his coaching career. The mountain he mounts determines who sees him and calls him for better opportunities. Another point is passing the ball backwards, which might enable the defender to score an own goal. This could ruin the effort of the team, which might apologise for the error and the damage done, but the head coach or manager would take responsibility in the long run by providing answers to questions being asked by the team's shareholders and stakeholders regarding the future of the team. This is a serious issue based on the outcome of the loss match, which is a result of the backward pass made by the careless defender. In most cases, it might lead to his appointment being terminated and it might take him a while to get another team to manage. However, his exit at his previous team might have a negative impact to a certain extent when entering into negotiations with his new club. The situation might leave the head coach with no choice. "We know you can do the job, but our fear is your performance at the previous team you managed, but if you prove yourself within a time frame, we might adjust your terms and conditions."

Another point is that the defender might remain a team member after the coach's dismissal, and later becomes the head coach, or might get another team or club to sign him to a better contract. *The end justifies the means;* the defender's error might reflect the head coach or manager as incapable of handling the team's success. However, the team manager's ability to remain decisive, accurate, and realistic before and during the match would reflect his strength as a better one, because he would have made the necessary adjustment, which was the best point to prove his strength before things felt apart.

With the total support of team members, it's possible for leaders to make use of their strengths to achieve goals within a short while, having identified the specific goal and discussed within the team how the goal is intended to be achieved. However, before a leader can leverage his strength in any situation, there is a need to figure out who each player is to identify their unique capabilities. I do advise my clients to stop thinking and fearing their weaknesses, but rather delegate them and learn from those whom they delegate to, to improve themselves, and to capitalize more on their strengths and their impact.

Be thankful for what you have; you'll end up having more. If you concentrate on what you don't have, you will never, ever have enough." ~ Oprah Winfrey

Taking an insight from the above quote, it becomes clearer to me that for anyone to excel at anything it's not enough to think about how best improve on one's weaknesses, rather, seek ways of leveraging one's strengths by being consistent at maintaining peak performance and remaining the best in whatever you do. Leaders need to seek feedback from various stakeholders to identify areas for improvement. However, it is important for leaders to invest in their strengths by finding ways to further develop their current skills and knowledge by reading books relating to their field, participating in training, workshops, and conferences.

CHAPTER 8

PLATFORMS FOR UTILIZING

ONE'S STRENGTH

To remain in a leadership position within any given industry and maintain peak performance, there is a need for leaders to continuously seek a platform for improvement. This requires the use of their strengths to create a positive environment, culture, and realistic relationship with relevant stakeholders to produce successful results to claim the edge over competitors. In a nutshell, the required areas for utilizing one's strength include the following:

TEAM BUILDING

A leader's strength will always go a long way towards building teams to help execute organisational strategies. Team building is a platform for leaders to create an environment of trust, compassion, stability, and fairness. It's paramount for any leaders' strengths to include the ability to communicate and connect with stakeholders. The ability to communicate effectively enables leaders to handle any form of discord and dispute among stakeholders, provided they remain unbiased.

Thus, relationship building within and outside an organisation is one of the most important strengths that a leader needs to process to enable the creation of collaborative goals, and develop a platform for supporting each other, especially when taking risk during tough times.

Effective leaders need to recognise the importance of building solid relationships while spending a reasonable amount of time focusing their efforts on key areas which requires improvements. A solid relationship makes it easier for leaders to connect with the people they lead via three simple tools.

1   **LISTENING**: It's wise for leaders to let others speak while they pay attention to issues being deliberated on. This removes anything that would distract from their conversations, and focuses on what people are trying to convey. From my experience as a coach, people appreciate being given the chance to tender their concerns. In a nutshell, leaders find it easier to read the state of their members' minds when they listen more. It helps in building the right platform with effective decision making within an organisation.

Being the leader does not mean that one man owns the team members. This should be noted by any leader who wishes to receive a healthy level of respect from his employees. Hence, the most important thing about listening to teammates is that they are the only ones able to advise or correct situations if things go wrong, for which the leaders typically take the whole blame. Furthermore, listening would transform any team's performance, if leaders could wisely make friends with their team member to connect, and get the best work out of them.

I remember my former superior, while I was a council environmental officer many years ago; he made friends with us officers. He often bought us chicken and chips, and at times pizza, while we all shared, joked and laughed, but I noticed one particular thing later. While sharing those happy moments, he wisely made his requests after calling our attention to an existing issue or task to be carried out within a time frame in which we all cooperate to help achieve the expected target.

2   **UNDERSTANDING**: Leaders need to appreciate

the effort of others, and also value their contributions. This ability in leaders to reflect a selfless approach in their relationship with others makes the job more interesting due to the positive impact that is created. This is because understanding a leader's relationship creates an emotional feeling that the leader is on the side of team members. Having a good level of understanding helps to keep an organisation's rate of turnover down in the long run. Sharing a good level of understanding among team members and other stakeholders enables leaders to not only remain open to new ideas, but maintain eagerness to learn new things.

3   ACKNOWLEDGEMENT: Leaders need to acknowledge the contributions of others in attaining excellence performance, because a tree can never make a forest. Leaders need to learn and know how to give credit to team members for their successes attained at various levels of an operational process. A bird in hand is better than a hundred in the bush. Leader should at any point in time cherish and motivate their members, and most of all, those ready to go the extra mile to make success a reality. This prompts them to remain motivated to remain industrious and innovative.

Building relationships enables leaders to understand more about influencing strategies, and what influence is at various stages, i.e., helping leaders in challenging the assumption that creates a negative impact about the future of members within the organisation at a glance. This includes inspiring others by supporting and encouraging them through tough times, and also giving assurances of a better future.

Building a better relationship is one thing, and maintaining it is another, so therefore leaders need to continuously improve their influence and negotiation skills to enable them to remain at their peak. Developing an action plan, and applying relevant concepts and processes would enable leaders to remain synchronized with their team members.

STRATEGIC AND CRITICAL THINKING

It is expected of every leader to think and act strategically, which is a critical leadership skill. The ability to think and act strategically enhances the effectiveness of a leader during a strategy implementation processes. Leaders who think strategically constantly assess their external environment and other parameters that could affect the organisation in both the long and short run. They think ahead to situations that could occur as a result of current industry trends, mostly in areas of change, such as customers' taste, legislation and fashion.

Both strategic and critical thinking are useful parameters in evaluating an organisation's corporate strategy to survive competition and maintain a leadership position within an industry. That way of thinking is also relevant in analysing information and other internal challenges at the department level of an organisation in achieving expected results. However, strategic thinking needs to be an on-going process, because it's an essential problem-solving tool to use in tackling everyday business challenges. Hitting it home, organisational success rests in the hands of competent leaders and executives who possess analytical skills and problem-solving skills, which require the ability to examine problems and opportunities critically, and implement solutions in response to market competition to improve the overall performance of their organisation. It is wise for leaders to bear in mind that effective problem solving begins with a realistic definition of the problem to be handled by applying a set of proven approaches for rational and creative problem-solving.

Some other benefits of both strategic and critical thinking are the provision of an accurate platform for diagnosing business issues, generating options, and implementing solutions in an innovative manner. However, knowing or having the solution to a problem is different from implementing or applying the same solution to get an accurate or expected result is another. They both help in making strategic decisions, which help leaders in the clarification and generating of various options and criteria under challenging conditions.

In terms of improving strategic and critical thinking skills, leaders have to work on their strengths in terms of thinking creatively, by generating alternatives, visualizing new possibilities, challenging assumptions, and opening themselves to new information and techniques, which include welcoming reasonable ideas from others.

In a nutshell, developing the ability of strategic thinking is about having clear insights about markets, customers, technology, and new information on emerging realities to develop a significant point of view about the future.

STRATEGIC EXECUTION

Most people confuse the terms strategic planning and execution, in both theory and practise. Strategic planning is telling or forecasting what an organisation intends to do, while strategic execution is doing what an organisation has initially forecasted, i.e., bringing spoken ideals to action, which makes it realistic to link people, strategies, and operations. Actions speak louder than words, a popular saying which reflects the capability of a leader in the presence of stakeholders. In practise, strategic planning does not on its own boost the strength of a leader, because it's only about expectations regarding a potential situation in which the plan might face challenges, obstacles, and setbacks. Thus, the exhibition of the required strength and ability to overcome barriers in executing the initial plan reflects more of what a leader can do, especially when faced by unexpected situations which might lead them to fold up plans, makes one a strong leader. A leader's strength and knowledge in execution makes it easier to carry others along while making choices and decisions, mostly in terms of implementing change within an organisation.

Having coached topics related to strategic planning and

execution over the years, I tell my clients to always consider three paramount factors in strategic execution, regardless of the industry they operate, i.e., strategic alignment, which is the process and the result of linking an organisation's structure and resources with its strategy and business environment. Breaking it down, an organisation's structure pertains to both reporting and operational relationships, with some degree of permanence in function and expectations. However, organisational resources are the major components within an organisation used in accomplishing goals, which include human, financial, physical, and informational resources. Leaders are mainly responsible for the overseeing, acquiring and managing the resources to accomplish goals by avoiding wastage.

However, gaining commitment is often the end-product of connecting with people to help in achieving one's vision. Drawing insight from John C. Maxwell's book, *Everyone Communicates, Few Connect*, he made it clear that for leaders to succeed, they must learn how to connect with people, and he went further in sharing the Five Practices to develop the crucial skills of connecting with others, which includes; finding common ground, keeping communication simple, capturing people's interest, inspiring people and staying authentic in all. Gaining others' commitment within an organisation requires the leader's ability to remain authentic in all their relationships, and avoid pretending.

In terms of translating strategy into action, leaders need to employ the right skills and competence for execution, which includes the effective management and clarification of an organisation's culture in achieving success. Aligning organisational capability for the purpose of success includes the processes and planning of various methods for improvement with an organisation's system at both departmental and sectional levels. However, the major benefits of the three platforms are positive outcomes in terms of aligning organisational performance for success, effective decision making, the ability to drive execution within an organisation, establishing the right strategic direction, and the ability to lead change.

These platforms enable leaders to have clear, specific strategic priorities, accountability and measures for achieving success. Another fact is it helps in the identification of core and job/role competencies required for high performance within teams and organisations, and systems that help or hinder strategy execution.

It's wiser for leaders to cite strategic execution as a top priority which requires a realistic framework to facilitate, convince, support, and gain understanding from stakeholders in terms of achievement. Otherwise, a leader might run from pillar to post to get things done as expected.

CHAPTER 9

THE ROLE OF STRENGTH IN
LEADERSHIP

In conclusion, without any small print, leadership requires strength to execute and deliver an excellent result, and to inspire others regarding the big picture. It also requires vulnerability. In most cases, the only option left for leaders is to carry an organisation on and strengthen its relationships with its stakeholders. This is a way of gaining their commitment to move the organisation forward.

Strength is a major requirement in the development of others, which has remained a major challenge for leaders. In making organisational values more visible and viral, leaders need to let others know what they stand for. However, what an organisation stands for reflects its values, integrity, diversity, and commitment to community development and service.

There's nothing more rewarding than leaders seeing the advancement of their organisation, and the growth, development, and improvement of others. It requires the use extraordinary strength to make others understand the key skills of leadership. The leader's strength is a platform to build and maintain high-performance leadership, which serves as the flagship of every successful leader. This includes the ability to lead team members, and carry other stakeholders along in times of change fearlessly, being and remaining resourceful, decisive, straightforward and composed. Leaders do whatever it takes in employing a participative management style to help build and maintain strategic relationships which help build a successful profile.

However, the strength of a leader enables him to remain focused in light of knowing his direction, and what's he is doing, how to do it and when to do it. He is aware of his own strengths by knowing those things he does well and enjoys doing, those things he learns fast and integrates into his wisdom naturally. A reasonable leader puts his strengths to use to assess his performance, and seeks ways for improvement. The strength of a leader makes him confident and comfortable with ambiguity, because he now knows and understands more about what it takes to a leader. Regardless of the size of the organisation, no leader can get it done alone, regardless of his qualification, skills or wisdom. He will always need to reach out for the support of others who can provide initiatives. To be successful, an organisation should always flourish, survive industrial competition, and maintain a good position within the market as a result of a high level of integrity, commitment to goals and the ability to connect with others, which fosters the maximum use of their strengths.

High-performance leadership is about a leader possessing the ability to first clarify his vision and strategy toward satisfying the needs of the stakeholders of an organisation, by giving performance improvement major consideration at all levels in an organisation. No man is an island of knowledge, so therefore leaders should always learn and seek ways to improve their skills, and never see themselves as the best among equals, regardless of their recorded achievements, because one man's best clothes are another man's rags. One man's account balance is another man's donation at a function. However, the total length of one's knowledge and skills might be a portion of another. Therefore, being highly effective in teams of performance requires continuous learning and improvement and not depending one's current knowledge and skill. There is always room for improvement.

www.ingramcontent.com/pod-product-compliance
Lightning Source LLC
Chambersburg PA
CBHW051228200326
41519CB00025B/7291